D1559213

*You
Can't
Judge
a Book
by Its
Cover*

# You Can't Judge a Book by Its Cover

## Marvin Kitman

WEYBRIGHT AND TALLEY
NEW YORK

*For Harold Robbins, Jacqueline Susann, Helen
Gurley Brown, Hugh Heffner, and Carol Kitman*

AC
8
.K778

220951

# CONTENTS

*You
Can't
Judge
a Book
by Its
Cover*

*Introduction:*
*How I*
*Became a*
*Renaissance*
*Man in My*
*Spare Time*

A woman in a tweed pants suit came up to me at a party recently and asked, "What do you do?" I told her that I spent all my time writing magazine articles. "Man," she said, "you're really in a bag."

"Sir?" I asked politely, as she started to edge away.

After the same embarassing thing happened several times that night, I confided in a friend who seemed to understand the scene. "What's wrong with me?"

There are some things even a friend won't tell you. But apparently this wasn't one of them. He blurted it right out: "You're not what's happening today, baby."

"If you mean I have to start letting my hair grow," I said, "forget it. That's okay for you guys with straight hair, but I'd wind up looking like Shirley Temple."

"All the beautiful people today," he continued, telling it to me the way it is, "are mixing media. Andy Warhol is a painter who's making films. Tom Wolfe is a writer who draws. Robert Rauschenberg is a painter composing electronic music. George Plimpton is a quarterback who plays triangle with the New York Philharmonic. You've got to get yourself another bag." I laughed at him.

I've lived through fads before. I missed out on the excitement of the Beat Generation, for example, when my mother wouldn't let me go hitchhiking. I could sit this one out, too, until men who did one thing well came into fashion at cocktail parties again. But I read in the papers a few days later that what's happening in the arts today is the second Renaissance. The first Renaissance lasted over two hundred years. I couldn't bear the thought of being a nobody at parties that long.

When I ran into my friend the hippie at another party the following weekend, I explained, "I want to be what's happening. How do I get with it, man?"

"Find your thing," he advised.

"My *what*?"

"Blow your mind," he said. "Try everything and see what turns you on." What gave me the courage to try to become a Renaissance man was a story in *Life* magazine about the discovery of the lost notebooks of Leonardo da Vinci. The master had set down his ideas and visions on the usual wide variety of subjects, including art, the flight of birds, weapons, obscure riddles and ball bearings. It reminded me of my own early notebooks.

Lost now since the 1930s and 1940s, the hardcovered "composition" notebooks from grammar school days at P.S. 186 in Brooklyn were filled with sketches of military inventions such as death rays. At ages eleven and twelve, like Leonardo, I was very much interested in anatomy, setting down my unique ideas on the subject in a series of drawings of classmates Selma and Marilyn without their clothes on. My sketches of giant hamburgers and Coke bottles, drawn as the lunch hour approached, anticipated developments in art. While others wrote down lines from Robert Louis Stevenson to memorize for poetry-appreciation class, I saw beauty in things around me. I still remember the first stanza of one of the environmental poems in my notebook:

*Have you tried Wheaties?*

*They're whole wheat with all of the bran.*
*Won't you try Wheaties?*
*For wheat is the best food of man.*
*They're crispy and crunchy the whole year through.*
*Jack Armstrong never tires of them and neither will you.*
*So just buy Wheaties,*
*The best breakfast food in the land.*

In those days, my mind had no boundaries. The only problem now was picking out my thing.

I decided to try novel writing first. Every writer, I had been hearing for years, has at least one novel in him. Aware of my technical limitations—I had never written fiction before—I decided to study with the masters in my spare time. I sent in a coupon to enroll in the fiction course at the Famous Writers School of Westport, Connecticut.

Several days later, the aptitude test, which weeded out applicants whose talent wasn't worth developing, arrived at Kitman House in Leonia, New Jersey. I answered the easy questions first:

Q. Name your three favorite authors.
A. Jacqueline Susann, Harold Robbins, Irving Wallace.
Q. What do you hope to achieve as a writer?
A. My goal is to write a first novel that the critics will call "promising." I also would like to clear 1.5 mil on paperback and movie rights.

But I got hung up on the essay question: "Tell of an experience you have had at some time in your life—any kind of experience you feel a reader would be interested in." Rather than bore famous writers such as Bruce Cat-

**3**

ton, Bennett Cerf, Rudolf Flesch, Bergen Evans and Faith Baldwin with anything from my dull present life, I decided to write about the kind of experience I hoped to have once I became a Renaissance man. I copied a few paragraphs verbatim from pages 194 and 195 of my favorite literary work, *Valley of the Dolls*, giving it an original twist by writing in the first person and by changing the characters' names from Jennifer and Tony to Selma and Marvin.

My hands stroked her breasts. My fingers fumbled with the buttons on her satin robe. "Jesus . . . why do you wear robes with buttons?" I pulled the robe off her shoulders, down to her waist. I stood back, my breath coming faster.

"Selma, no one should have boobs like that." I touched them lightly.

She smiled. "They're yours, Marvin."

I buried my face in them, sinking to my knees. "Oh, God. I just can't believe it. Every time I touch them, I can't believe it." My mouth was greedy. . . .

"Marvin, let's get married."

"Sure, baby, sure. . . ." I was fumbling at the rest of the buttons on her robe. It fell to the floor. She backed away. I crawled on my knees after her. She backed away again.

"Marvin, all of this"—she stroked her body— "is *not* yours . . . it's *mine!*"

I came after her. She eluded me again. She stroked her thighs, her fingers touching between her legs. "That's mine, too," she said softly. "But *we* want you, Marvin," she whispered hoarsely. "Take your clothes off. . . ."

And so forth, for two more pages.

Before I got around to mailing the test, which had been sent to me "without obligation," a member of the faculty of the Famous

4

Writers School called and said he just happened to be in New Jersey and would be stopping by to mark my test in person. I looked forward to having an intelligent discussion with the visiting professor on technical matters.

"How does the Famous Writers School recommend writing a best seller," I asked, "with a manual or an electric typewriter?" He said subject matter was important, too. "That's why I want to write about sex and perversion," I explained.

"Surely, as a writer," he chuckled, "you wouldn't mind getting those big beautiful checks writing about other subjects, too, would you?"

I assured him that I also wanted to write about other forms of human depravity. "You know—grass, pot, Mary Jane, Acapulco gold, acid, freak-outs, blowing your mind. I want to tell it like it really is."

Every time I started to discuss Proust, Stendhal, Gide and Joyce and their influence on Burroughs, Genêt and Jackie Susann, he brought the subject back to money and how important it was for a writer to learn how to sell his stuff. "Do you teach novelists how to invent new art forms?" I asked. "My thing is something I call 'nonfiction fantasy.' "

He skimmed through the "Ability to Use Words" and "Grammar" sections of the test booklet but read somewhat slower when he reached the essay question. "You certainly capture the reader's interest here," he said. "You have a way with dialog . . . suspense builds . . . ear for language . . . terse style. . . ." Miss Su-

5

sann would be pleased to learn that her work was finally being praised at the academy level. "Frankly, this is almost pornographic."

"You're too kind," I said modestly.

Nearing the climax of the essay, he removed his glasses to wipe the steam off. "Holy mackerel," he said. "I know who you've been influenced by."

"Who?" I asked uneasily.

"You've been reading Mickey Spillane."

As far as I was concerned, the Famous Writers School had flunked the test. They didn't recognize good writing when they saw it. But my face fell anyway, when I saw my grade.

"C-plus is a very good mark," the visiting professor explained, "although not as good as B, which is superior. In all my experience, I've heard of only one writer getting an A." That must have been Leon Uris, I guessed. He said that I had a lot to learn about fiction but that the school would be willing to gamble on me anyway. For only $625, I could study the novel under a famous writer like Faith Baldwin.

Could Miss Baldwin, who hadn't written a best seller in years, teach me anything about sex, drugs and depravity? Could she give me the courage to use modern words like S**T or F**K? "She's not my bag," I told him bluntly.

In the half hour it took to get him out of the house, the Famous Writers School man spoke so highly of my raw talent that I decided to start working on my first novel that night. I wrote "Chapter One" on several pieces of paper. Everything was going according to schedule. I had developed the biggest writer's block on my street.

While thumbing through *Reader's Digest* in

search of advice on how to live with myself as a social failure, I came across an ad that began: "WE TEACH YOU HOW TO DRAW AND PAINT SUCCESSFULLY AT HOME." By the time I finished reading how the Famous Artists School of Westport, Connecticut, could teach anybody with talent how to earn money in his spare time, it occurred to me that perhaps my thing was art. That's where the action was today— and the bread. Besides, a man had to use only one piece of paper to create a masterpiece, and he could erase.

A visiting professor from the Famous Artists School arrived at my house several days after the art-talent test was sent to me "without obligation." I explained that I was interested in more than just drawing, painting or sculpting: I wanted to make a real statement with my art. He looked first at some of the statements I had made in the section of the talent test labeled "Tell Us About Yourself":

Q. Why would you like to become a good artist?
A. Make money; make the scene.
Q. Have you studied art? Where?
A. I browse in the soup and cleanser sections of the supermarket and read *Time* magazine regularly to learn what's happening in art.
Q. Which mediums interest you most?
A. I plan to major in human figures, but I also would like to work with auto bodies.

He said all my answers were right.

"How do I find subjects to draw for the Human Figures home-study course at Famous Artists?" I asked with some embarrassment. "Do you send the models over the state line from Connecticut?" It disturbed me to hear that I would have to find my own subjects.

"Well, do you at least teach students how to get girls to take off their clothes?" That would come with experience, he explained.

Everything went smoothly on the art-talent test until the faculty member looked at my drawings for the creative portion of the exam. Question three was called "Your Sense of Form." On the page was a large pencil sketch of a nude girl. The instructions were, "Complete the outlined figure by drawing a costume on it. Use an ordinary soft pencil to clothe the figure. Be sure to retain the feeling of the human form beneath the clothes." There were three examples of how the problem might be solved—all hopelessly square when compared with my rendering.

"I've seen ten thousand tests," the visiting professor said when he saw my creation, "but I've never seen anything like *that*." I had put a nun's coif and veil on the figure's head. Then I added a topless dress, black-mesh stockings and knee-high stainless-steel boots.

"I admit that it's not fully realized," I told the professor, "but it's meant to symbolize the ecumenical mood between spiritual and secular society."

"That's what you're trying to say here?"

"Well, sir, I wanted the figure to represent the modern church emerging, a real swinging nun. I call the genre 'pope art.'"

The master opened his black-leather portfolio and handed me a calendar published by the Hartford Insurance Group. The illustration for each month, he explained, had been done by a Famous Artists student in his spare time. "Wouldn't you rather paint like this and earn real money?"

Suspecting that this might be the art-appreciation part of the test, I put on a pair of midnight-blue sunglasses to see the calendar art better. The farm and seashore scenes still looked bilious. Then I flicked the light switch on and off to see if stroboscopic go-go lights helped. "No," I said finally. "You don't seem to understand. I want to be a *fine* artist, somebody like Andy Warhol, Jasper Johns, Claes Oldenburg, Roy Lichtenstein or Antonio Varga."

"What is it you admire in *those* people?"

"First of all, the high prices they get for their work. But I also admire their creative approaches to capital gains, reproduction rights, the way they write off travel expenses on their income-tax forms, their investments in oil wells and art galleries. . . ."

"There is an old saying in art," he said. "Before you can paint, you must learn how to draw. You cannot put the cart before the horse. You must learn the basics. Tell me, what have you *done* in art?"

I showed him the box of Rinso from my blue period, which I had made art by adding my signature. "What do you call this?" he asked.

"Some people call it art," I said. "But I'm not completely satisfied with it."

"Good. What do you think is wrong?"

"The signature should be larger." He was frowning. "What's the matter?" I asked. "Do you doubt the authenticity of this work?"

He quickly said, "No, no. I'm sure you did it yourself."

Then I pointed to my bull's-eye, a found object from an archery range in Paramus. "That's representative of my Robert Indiana period,"

9

I explained. "And this I call *Salami Sandwich*, from my lunch period." The only thing he seemed to be enthusiastic about was a childlike painting rich in strong primary colors, titled *Crude Oil*. "My son did that," I said coldly, steering him toward my first piece of modern sculpture, a broken-down club chair, an example of the art of destruction. "He also helped do this."

"Have you ever tried to draw people?" he asked.

*Zonk!* Another insult. I had answered the last question in the test booklet—"Make an original drawing or picture of any subject you wish in the space above"—with a portrait of Lamont Cranston, done in the Benday technique of one of America's great artists, Roy Lichtenstein. First I drew a frame bordering the rectangular space, then I added a plaque at the bottom in the shape of a comic-strip bubble, suitably inscribed: "WHO KNOWS WHAT EVIL LURKS IN THE HEARTS OF MEN?" But the symbolism escaped this so-called art expert.

"What is this?" he complained.

"There is actually less here than meets the eye," I explained patiently. "I drew Lamont Cranston at work as The Shadow." The visiting professor didn't say anything. "I hope this isn't your way of telling me the Famous Artists School thinks that what's popular today isn't art," I said angrily.

"You have a flair," he said, withdrawing a batch of admission forms from his portfolio. "You definitely have the talent. It would be criminal not to do something about it. We have twelve famous artists, men such as Jon Whitcomb and Norman Rockwell, ready to help you become a success. The complete course is only six hundred and twenty-five dollars."

"For that kind of bread, will your school teach me the fundamentals, like how to get Robert and Ethel Scull interested in my work, which are the best galleries to exhibit in and how to keep my prices up?" The visiting professor's silence was making me suspicious. "What *do* you teach at the Famous Artists School?" I asked.

The visiting professor marked my test B-minus. My grades were already so good, I told him, that I didn't see much point in going any further with the Famous Artists School. He had been so unstinting in praise of my ability that I felt like a child prodigy. They had nothing more to teach me.

But I didn't rest on my laurels. While waiting for an inspiration about what to draw, paint or sculpt, I turned on to something that combined all my talents—underground-film making. I screened the rushes of the home movies I had made over the years. Their slick commercial quality so depressed me that I wrote to Andy Warhol for pointers.

"Everybody's been saying they don't like your painting," began my letter to the old master, "but that you are a great film maker. Would it be possible for me to study the art of cinema with you? I especially want to take your course in shooting out of focus and making double exposures. What I have in mind is a feature based on my novel. I plan to film it by focusing the camera on the pages, beginning with Chapter One, page one, page two, and so

**11**

forth, without cutting a word. My goal is to make an uncompromising film, one that people will walk out on.

"P.S. I have my own hand-held camera."

The next day, a faculty member from a correspondence music school I'd written to stopped by the house to discuss my lessons in advanced piano and composition. "Do you know Chopin's Opus 9, Number 3?" he asked, as I sat down at the piano.

"I don't play Chopin."

"How about Rachmaninoff, then?"

"I don't play Rachmaninoff." After running through MacDowell, Saint-Saëns and Rossini, I finally made it clear to him that I played only the moderns—more specifically, John Cage, and then only his important work *4'33"*. "My ambition is to compose serious classical music like that," I explained. "In fact, I've just finished my first piece. May I play *Concerto Sinusoidal Wave on a Frequency of 20,000 Cycles Per Second in A-flat* for you?" I turned the tape recorder on. After a while, I asked, "Well, what's your professional opinion?"

"I didn't hear anything," he finally said, "except a dog howling out in your yard."

"That's the beauty of it. The reason he's howling is that I'm blowing a dog whistle. It's above the threshold of human hearing, of course, but with repeated listening, you may be able to feel it in your molars. Why don't you listen to the whole thing again?"

"That won't be necessary," he said. "Is that the only kind of music you're interested in learning?"

"Well, random sounds also turn me on."

He said he thought I could learn how to do

those things myself. I thanked him for his confidence.

Several days later, the phone rang in my study, where I was composing my *Symphony Number One*, which called for the musicians to sit idly by their instruments for an hour. I hoped it would be Mr. Warhol giving me an appointment to take my screen test or advising me to forget technique and concentrate on getting my first film entered in a festival. "This is the Fred Astaire Dance Studios," said a sultry woman's voice. "We have an important question to ask you. What was the name of the first President of the United States?"

"Booker T. Washington," I answered.

"That's close enough," she said breathlessly. "You've just won a free private one-hour dance lesson. This is your chance to learn the modern dance steps that may have been keeping you from achieving social success."

"I have a physical handicap."

"I'm so sorry," she said sympathetically. "Forgive me for calling."

"What I mean is, I have two left feet. Ever since I was a teenager, all the girls have been saying I'm hopeless. It would take a lifetime of lessons to teach me how to dance. I know your studio wouldn't want to get involved in long-term arrangements like that."

"If you can walk," she said, breathing hard, "we can teach you how to dance. When would you like your free lesson? Any time at your convenience."

Even a Renaissance man like Leonardo probably did the "in" dances, such as the tarantella, when he wasn't painting portraits or taking flying lessons. "I'll be tied up working on my novel, painting, composing my symphony and making my film until 11:30 P.M.," I explained. "Why don't you come over to my place about midnight?"

She said I would have to go to the Fred Astaire Dance Studio nearest my home to pick up my prize. But I couldn't find time during the next few days. What bothered me was how Renaissance men managed to keep all the arts straight in their minds. In some way, I had to learn how to organize my spare time, which by now was sheer chaos.

On my way over to the dance studio on the bus a few days later, I saw an ad in the paper for a kind of famous executives' school, called Mr. Executive, Inc., which claimed to teach bright young men all the shortcuts to the top in the business world, including how to budget their time effectively. Fortunately, a new course was starting that night at the Columbia University Club in New York and the ad offered a free first lesson. At that moment, capital gains seemed more important than the boogaloo, so I went off to gain administrative wisdom.

Our teacher—or group leader, as he called himself—explained to the men on their way up that psychologists have proven you have ten seconds to make a good impression at an interview. That is certainly true at a party. "At Mr. Executive, we teach you how to look like an executive, act like an executive and sound like an executive." I would need to know all those things when I started talking to the Rockefellers, the Guggenheims and the Fords about foundation subsidies to continue my studies in the arts. "While you're up," I'd be able to say firmly to the man interviewing me, "get me a grant."

The class was divided into "buzz groups" for brainstorming hypothetical problems. The object was to teach us how to freewheel, to unblock our minds, to think creatively. "At Mr. Executive," the group leader said enthusiastically, "we learn how to think smarter, not work harder."

I came up with the winning answer on the question of how to cure lateness at the plant: "Last man in the door blows the whistle."

Everybody also had to make a five-minute speech about himself. While listening to the other fellows talk about their things, I got to thinking about the similarities between business and art. Basically, we were all striving for the same thing: recognition. The faster we got it, the better. My classmates were all content to work their way up to the top of big corporations. But I wanted instant recognition. I needed a *shtick*. Suddenly it came to me: The fruition of my own private renaissance would be to open a boutique.

A boutique run by a Renaissance man like myself would soon become a mecca of wit and wisdom, a gathering place for the literary set, the art set, the television set. What would bring the customers in would be a massive mixed-media project: I could read aloud from my novel in progress; exhibit my paintings, drawings and sculpture; show my homemade movie —all at the same time. Even the classical-music crowd would be lured into the store by my John Cage recitals, non-played on a seventeenth-century harpsichord.

**15**

"Please advise if your firm would be interested in manufacturing the following line of clothes for my shop," I wrote to the president of Hart Shaffner & Marx: "(1) a six-button, double-breasted, pinch-back formal dinner jacket with sergeant's stripes and color-coordinated epaulets; (2) a disposable paper mourning suit for use at funerals or other occasions where black is appropriate; (3) a 'blazer,' or whatever less incendiary name the paper-fabric industry would call this type of sports jacket; (4) a business suit—an executive model made out of *Wall Street Journals*—for the man who wants to look like a million bucks; and (5) a raincoat of blotting paper. My boutique plans to carry a quality line of merchandise, so the materials should be of high rag content. They shouldn't show footprints and should be water-resistant enough so that a woman might still be able to cry on a man's shoulder."

"For your business suit," answered Claiborn M. Carr, Jr., president of one of the largest paper-fabric corporations, "perhaps the cuffs can be left starkly white for those in the habit of jotting notes; and, for those who don't take shorthand, a more extensive sleeve, ranging from wrist to midway between the elbow and the shoulder, can be left white."

I tried to find loopholes in my plans for the boutique, which I planned to call The Collected Papers of Marvin Kitman. Should paper suits go out of style, they'd still be useful as pot holders, as napkins or for polishing the sports car. The only obstacle standing in the way of the boutique's success seemed to be me. Nobody under thirty would trust me, because of my voice.

"IS YOUR SPEECH HOLDING YOU BACK?" asked an ad in *The New York Times* the next morning. "Dorothy Sarnoff, famed Broadway, opera and TV star, can give you the speech personality you've always wanted." I went over to her salon on the mezzanine of the Hotel St. Moritz to hear what the beautiful actress could do for me with her Speech Cosmetic Course.

"Say anything you like," she said, putting my voice on tape so we could analyze the problem together. Thinking about her musical-comedy background, the first thing that came to mind was: "The rain in Spain stays mainly on the plain. . . ." She suggested that I tell a story instead. I told her about my thing. There wasn't a wet eye in the house.

"Your problem is that you don't speak with authority," she explained. "What's missing in your voice is confidence. In the show-business sense, you don't have what we call *sell*."

"That's why I want to learn how to speak with an English accent."

"Noel Coward wouldn't be *you*," she laughed. I agreed with her: a Coward voice would be all right if I wanted to make it with the literati.

"The kind of accent I need to be effective in my boutique is a working-class-English accent. Can you teach me the East Liverpool sound?"

"People want to hear the real *you*," she said, shaking her head.

"Couldn't we use electronic-amplification sound equipment? The record companies do it all the time with kids from south Philadelphia."

**17**

"You'd be a phony."

I looked around to see who was calling me names. Most speech teachers work in drab rooms in office buildings. Miss Sarnoff's salon was filled with mock Louis XIV furniture, glass crystal chandeliers and mirrors with gold frames made of plaster of Paris. I realized that I could never get a groovy voice surrounded by such bad vibrations; Miss Sarnoff didn't even look like the kind person pictured in her newspaper ads. "I'll ring you up sometime," I said. "Cheery bye."

On the way back to Leonia that day, it struck me that the Kitman boutique would never work after all. Running a clothing store, even under such favorable mixed-media circumstances, would mean being face to face with hundreds of people each day; and who ever heard of a brilliant, sensitive artist being able to get along with anyone? Can you imagine one of the greats—Jim Morrison, for instance—asking whether the pants should break a little at the shoe tops, or maybe be without cuffs altogether? Of course not. Well, Kitman wouldn't stoop, either.

But my newly emerging talents were going to waste. Then, suddenly, the vast, rolling, inspirational Jersey Meadows turned me on. Eureka! North Beach! I had found my thing! I whipped out an old Baby Ruth wrapper carried in case of artistic emergency and deftly sketched the first new ad, complete with board of advisors and Connecticut farmhouse. I was ready to announce the first-semester curriculum of the Marvin Kitman Famous Renaissance Man School.

# PART ONE

# FEATS

## THE WORLD OF HIGH, MEDIUM & LOW FINANCE

I'll never forget the day I looked at the New York skyline, while riding into town on the bus from New Jersey, and thought, "Someday all that will be mine." But that was fifteen years ago, before I knew my limitations. Why couldn't I now settle for just a piece of Manhattan? Thumbing through a brochure for a recent Department of Real Estate auction of city-owned surplus property, I saw a parcel which seemed right up my alley.

At least I hoped it was an alley. The catalog said only that "Block 2176, Lot 2, Borough of Manhattan" was a vacant lot, measuring two feet wide by one hundred feet deep.

A private alley is a wonderful status symbol

*My Slice of the Real-Estate Pie*

**19**

for a man who grew up on the sidewalks of New York. Whenever the spirit moved me, I'd be able to go back to my land. I could kick a rusty can around, hit stones with a broomstick or just lean against a wall watching the sun glint off broken bottles—without harassment from landlords or tenants. Nobody would be able to break up my stickball game or pour a pot of hot water down on me for making noise, because I was the owner of the alley. I went over to the ballroom of the Hotel Roosevelt, where the Real Estate Department conducts land auctions to see if I could really afford a piece of Manhattan.

The upset price, or the minimum the city would take for the parcel, was $25. Because of its choice location—near the corner of Fort Washington Avenue and West 177th Street—I ran into competition from developers. After a dramatic bidding battle, the auctioneer finally knocked down the parcel in my name for $40.

"Cheer up," said an old man sitting near me in the crowded ballroom. "I've bought slivers before. You can't be sure about the size. It can't be any smaller than the catalog says, but it could be a lot bigger."

I followed the sliverlord's advice and went to City Hall to look up my holdings on the municipal tax map. The records indicated my site actually measured 2 feet, 3/8 inch wide by 100.9 feet deep. To celebrate the windfall, I took the rest of the day off and went uptown to walk my land.

I found it between two apartment buildings, five and six stories high, in the historic Washington Heights section of town. A man asked me what I thought I was doing poking around in his back yard.

"Sir?"

"I got some complaints from tenants that a stranger was prowling around here. It's making them nervous."

"I'm the new owner," I said in a friendly manner.

"Of what?" he asked.

With a sweep of my hand, which I scraped against the bricks of the lefthand building, I pointed to my holdings. He threatened to call the cops if I didn't get out of there.

When I showed him the bill of sale from the city, he took several steps back. "You bought *that*?"

"It's all mine," I said proudly. "Do you mind telling me who put up this wall?"

Right in the middle of my dream alley was a retaining wall that appeared to be holding up the newer of the apartment houses. It was an eyesore and a hazard.

"I only work here," said the man, who claimed to be the janitor. He gave me the names of the two owners, both absentee landlords like myself. I put up a sign on the wall, reading No Ball Playing Allowed. The Owner, and unhappily went back to the suburbs.

For some reason the lawyer who handled my routine legal problems was very excited when he heard about the encroachment on my land. "Your property rights are being violated," he said. "You're lucky. Just let me handle it. You're going to make money on this deal."

I sensed I might be in the hands of one of

those slick operators who are always buying and selling Manhattan. "Whatever you're planning," I said, "count me out. I just want to use my land without tripping over a wall."

"Don't worry about a thing," he said. "When did you want to start using it?"

"Well, I was hoping to get away for the weekend."

The next thing I knew I received copies of letters the lawyer sent to my two new neighbors, which concluded: "Please get your building's foundation off my client's property at your convenience by 6:30 P.M Friday."

Later the lawyer called to ask if I had insurance.

"Look, I don't want to get involved in any trouble. Maybe I ought to sell."

He told me not to be a sap. Once he finished negotiating with the neighbors, if I still wanted to sell, I could get a reasonable profit, about twenty times my investment. "I'm just making sure you're protected for liability."

"How much will a policy cost?"

"The only company that will handle such an odd lot as yours is Lloyd's of London. It'll cost a few pounds, but it'll be worth it. And I'd set up an *ad hoc* realty corporation to develop your holdings."

"But the land is only worth forty dollars."

"Wise up," he explained. "Your property is only a block from Broadway."

"But it's only 24⅜ inches wide," I said, trying to keep a toehold on reality.

"That's plenty for a billboard," he explained.

The lawyer called again the next day. "Good news," he said. "You're going to let the neighbors know that you're planning to develop the property. It will help if they think you're considering a building."

"What did you have in mind?" I asked coldly.

"I was thinking of something along the lines of the world's narrowest skyscraper. I wrote to I. M. Pei & Associates in your name. Pei has a reputation for never turning his back on an architectural challenge."

Two days later the lawyer said he had heard from the architect. "Pei's office says he's out of town. You'd better get right over so we can discuss our next move."

As he spoke about new developments in lightweight construction materials, I began having visions of buying up other pieces of Manhattan and becoming the Tishman of the sliverworld. During our conference one of the neighbors finally called about his letter. The man was shouting so loudly on the phone, I could overhear snatches of the conversation. "Go ahead and tear down the wall," he said. "But if your client touches one brick of my building, I'll sue for every cent he's worth." My lawyer asked for a moment to consult with his client.

"He's the guilty party," the lawyer said happily. "We'll tell him we're sending over the bulldozer."

"If the retaining wall comes down," I explained, "so will his building."

Our conference was interrupted by the neighbor's voice. "I know who your client is," he was screaming. "It's the guy who owns the next-door building. Who else would buy that piece of junk?" My lawyer denied the allegation. Much to my surprise, he didn't threaten

**23**

to sue the man for calling my land bad names.

After the man hung up, my lawyer was jubilant. "We'll get an injunction forcing him to remove his encroachment forthwith. You're in great shape."

I didn't come down to asphalt until he began outlining some of the the costs of my legal triumph. I would have to pay two hundred dollars for a land survey, and to keep up the pressure on my neighbors, it would be necessary to commission the architect to draw up rough plans for the building. Even if I. M. Pei turned over the project to a junior associate, the fee would run into thousands. And I shuddered to think about what my lawyer's time was worth. I finally decided how to get out of the cul-de-sac.

"It has long been my belief," I wrote to Mayor John Lindsay, "that real-estate interests have a special obligation to help make New York, in your own words, 'a fun city.' Toward this end, I have decided to lease to the city a parcel of land, officially known as Block 2176, Lot 2, Borough of Manhattan. There are many social, cultural or practical purposes for which this parcel is suited, such as a natural vest-pocket park, a municipal parking lot for motor scooters, a *boccie* court, an archery range or a little City Hall. The land is ready for immediate occupancy, once you level the site."

The average person who owns a share of American business—Wall Street jargon for "playing the market"—is either a bull or a bear. He buys and sells haphazardly for the short or long run, depending on the way the market looks. But the really smart investors are in a third group of ultraconservatives called chickens. We never make a move in the market unless we are covered for every contingency. I had the opportunity to explain this theory to a customers' man at Merrill Lynch, Pierce, Fenner & Smith who had been calling me for a year, asking to handle my brokerage account. "Do you have any special investment problems I can help you solve?" he finally asked on the phone one day. "No," I explained, "I'm just afraid of being wiped out by peace." "Your fears are premature," he said confidently. "You haven't bought stock yet."

Account executives are not supposed to talk politics with their customers. So I assumed this was his nonpolitical way of attacking the sincerity of President Johnson's peace offensive, then roaring full blast. The White House had just announced it was resuming the bombing of North Vietnam and considering sending twenty-five thousand fresh troops to South Vietnam. But I knew this was only a smoke screen for the President's peace effort.

My customers' man assured me it was always smart to own a share of American business. I asked if he had heard Pope Paul's depressing speech at the U.N. "The Pontiff predicted, 'War no more; war never again.' Can Merrill Lynch give me any assurances that peace won't be hell?" He explained that the research department felt there was absolutely

*The First National Fiduciary Imperialist Trust Syndicate Cartel Pool Combine*

**25**

no chance there would be peace in our time. Apparently it was Merrill Lynch's view that as an investor I had nothing to fear but fear itself. I had heard from other usually reliably informed sources, however, that the Pope was infallible.

President Johnson's peace objective was for capitalism to triumph all over the world, thus creating a great society of peacefully competing rival capitalist economies, a kind of big ranch system in the sky. It finally occurred to me that I could have a hedge against peace, while supporting the President's program, by becoming the first person on my block in Leonia, New Jersey, to own a share of Russian business.

J. Paul Getty once said the only way to make money in the market is to buy when everybody else is selling. Everybody had been selling tsarist securities since 1917 for a sound reason. Investors' loss of confidence, I read in Sylvia Porter's influential syndicated column, had been caused by a decree issued by the All-Union Central Executive Committee in 1918 and later ratified by the Council of People's Commissars in 1920: "Absolutely, and without exception, all foreign loans are annulled."

But every American schoolboy knew you couldn't trust anything the Russians ever said, especially now that they seemed to be losing some of that old revolutionary spirit. An obscure Russian economics professor, I read in the newspapers, had just discovered the profit motive. The Supreme Soviet at its last session (1966) ratified the law of supply and demand. It was only a short dialectical leap forward to project which further contradiction in Marxist-

Leninist doctrine already might be in the works:

1968. Annulment of foreign loans unannulled. According to Sylvia Porter, Marshal Tito in 1957 resumed partial debit payments on the Yugoslavian Royal family's bonds, in default twenty-seven years to smooth the way for U.S. aid. A similar *rapprochement* might take place when the U.S. resumed lend-lease shipments to Moscow for use in its coming war with China.

*1972.* Foreign bondholders invited back to Russia to help current management squeeze a little extra profit out of workers.

*1973.* Leningrad Stock Exchange reopens. State Exchange Commission grants franchise to Merrill Lynch to open branch customers' rooms in factories and communes.

*1974.* Hero of Soviet Union medal goes to first American investor. *The Wall Street Journal* wins the Lenin Prize for business literature.

*1975.* Chamber of Deputies votes to change name to Chamber of Commerce.

*1976.* Communism itself withers away.

I began my crash program by going to a bank to raise the necessary working capital. An officer of the high-prestige Morgan Guaranty Trust Company's Fifth Avenue branch listened to a few of my anti-Roosevelt remarks designed to soften him up. "This isn't a retail bank that lends money to anybody who walks in off the street," the investment-banking-house executive finally said. "But we do make exceptions. What is your occupation?"

"I guess you would call me an industrialist."

"Do you work for anybody?"

I explained that I had just quit my job as a

writer to play the market full time. "That's what I need the money for. I'm taking a little flier in a real growth situation—the Russian bond market." He looked a little concerned, so I assured him I wasn't expecting to make a quick killing on tsarist bonds; they were strictly a long-term investment, or "red chips." "As a conservative investor," I added, "I'm going to limit my purchases to only those tsarist issues recommended by a reputable banker."

He asked for an example. Fortunately, I had found an old brochure in my grandmother's house urging Americans to buy Russian war bonds in 1916. The Imperial Russian Government Short-Term War Loan 5½ percent of 1916 had been highly touted by both J. P. Morgan and Company and the Guaranty Trust Company; before they merged, the two banking houses were the tsar's fiscal agents in the U.S. The banker coldly studied the glowing praise his predecessors had heaped on the war bonds. "Do you mind telling me what kind of collateral you're planning to use?" he asked.

"Well, I have an unpublished manuscript on how to make money in the market."

There was an embarrassing silence. I guessed he had seen some of my work as a writer and didn't like my style. "I'll pass your application on to the board," he said. "I'm sure they'll give it the full consideraton it deserves."

As a hedge, I also approached another leading investment banking house. "I bring you fraternal greetings from the capitalists of Leonia, New Jersey," I wrote to the small-loan manager of the State Bank of the U.S.S.R. in Moscow. After listing my financial requirements, I explained that the money would be used for the purchase of government bonds, not to feed my polo ponies. "As for references, our FBI has a complete dossier on all Americans who may someday do business with your government. I suggest one of your agents check my file on his regular weekly visit to FBI headquarters in Washington. My credit can also be established at the Russian Tea Room in New York City, where I have a charge account."

I quietly moved into the market by opening an account with the Merrill Lynch customers' man who had first given me the tip to buy Russian bonds. "I'll start off with railroads," I said, remembering all the time I had spent on troop trains in the peacetime Army.

"I'm glad you realize defense spending is bound to continue," the account executive said optimistically in the crowded Wall Street board room. "American railroads are always a sound investment."

"You don't understand. I want to buy Grand Russian Railroad Company 3 percent of 1869."

I had been tipped off about the Grand Russian while reading Tolstoy's *Anna Karenina*. The novel ends with the heroine throwing herself in front of one of the Grand Russian's crack trains. But I wasn't buying into the company because of the romance of Russian railroading. While thumbing through a book in the public library on the world's great railroads, I discovered Grand Russian Railroad still had 103 years remaining on its franchise to operate the Nicholas Line (now the October Line), the main trunk between Moscow and Leningrad. But the issue didn't seem to be my account executive's glass of vodka.

"Stay away from Grand Russian 3s," he was

shouting. I promptly assured him I was going to diversify my portfolio with other stocks. "Buy East-Ural Railroad Company 4½ percent of 1912 and Trans-Caspian Railway 3½ percent of 1879." My broker's face turned borscht red. He obviously hadn't done his homework here, either. The three railroads were key links in the Trans-Siberian network. East-Ural held the franchise for the Berdyaush-Lysva section; Trans-Caspian owned the right of way farther down the line, between Tashkent and Samarkand. Steppe by steppe, I planned to buy into all the *ad hoc* corporations the tsar established by ukase to build and operate the world's largest railway.

"The way you said you were worried about the market," he was yelling, "I thought you were a cautious investor. Everybody on the Street knows that stuff is the worst junk."

"Wall Street has been wrong before," I said, proving that I had done my economic homework by giving him the first figures that came to mind. "Remember 1929?" Then I headed over to the parlor section of the board room to watch my first transactions appear on the Trans-Lux screen.

"A small investor like you," he called after me, "should stick to government bonds."

"Buy Imperial Russian Government Three-Year Credit 6½ percent of 1916," I ordered from my shopping list. "And now that you're finally recommending things, do you have anything good in a Russian gold-mining stock? As an investor, I like current management's no labor costs in the mines."

"Well, what quality are we talking about in

the Imperial 6½s?" he asked. "One-hundred, five-hundred or one-thousand lots?"

Bonds are sold in thousand-dollar (par value) lots, the customers' man explained. He dialed Merrill Lynch's bond trader to order one lot's worth of Imperial 6½s for my account. "I forgot to mention," I added. "I want to buy everything on margin." The account executive patiently explained that a customer had to put up two thousand dollars in cash or securities as a deposit to open a margin account. So I ordered a second thousand of Imperial 6½s to cover the margin requirements. "And while you have the trader on the phone, I want to buy a few other red chips for my portfolio: Lithuanian Match Monopoly 4¾ percent of 1932, City of Greater Prague 6 percent of 1922, Austro-Hungarian Empire Iron Gate Loan 3 percent of 1895, City of Riga 4½ percent Loan of 1914 and Hungarian Cooperative Society Established for Financial Liquidation of Land Reform External Sinking Fund 5½ percent of 1929."

My thinking about owning a share of Lithuanian business, Czechoslovakian business, Latvian business and Hungarian business was also sound. Karl Marx once predicted about the future for capitalists in Russia, "The rich will get richer and the poor will get poorer." But I wasn't so naïve an investor to bank on anything Marx said. The Communist world had already split two for one on what he said about coexistence with the West. By diversifying my portfolio with securities from all the Iron Curtain countries, including Cuba and China, no future ideological conflict would be a total loss to me as an investor.

But my customers' man slammed down the phone receiver on its cradle. "That's it," he hissed like an overheated samovar. "I'm closing your account. It's for your own protection. You're going to lose your shirt."

"Your fears are premature," I said. "You haven't bought anything for me yet. But you did take my orders; commission them. And be sure to check the latest quotes on the Imperial 6½s. The price might have gone up." When he insisted it was bad business for Merrill Lynch to get involved in this kind of action, I began to suspect the nation's largest brokerage house had a Trotskyite on its sales force.

I demanded to see one of Merrill Lynch's ninety-one vice presidents, preferably one who wasn't soft on communism. He brought the branch manager instead. The comrade told me to take my tsarist speculations elsewhere. "Never sell the tsar short," I cried, carried away partly by emotion and partly by the Pinkerton the manager had summoned to remove me from the premises.

I followed the manager's advice anyway, by taking my business to another one of Merrill Lynch's 165 branch offices. There, a militantly anti-Communist account executive bought for my account $1,000 worth of Imperial 6½s. The price was $30. I immediately registered with the State Department as an imperialist agent.

"Our foreign policy calls for trading with the Communists," I wrote Dean Rusk in Washington. "Since I am now financially backing the 'outs'—the revolutionaries who want to overthrow the existing economic system in the Soviet Union—can I be prosecuted under the Trading with the Enemy act?"

State's Office of the Legal Advisor answered, "Transactions with either the U.S.S.R. or opponents of the present government are outside the scope of the act." But I was warned not to buy North Vietnam or Chinese securities.

Before increasing my holdings further, as a technical student of the market it was natural that I turn to an investment consultant for some advice. I found a fortuneteller listed in the yellow pages of the phone book. "Many businessmen consult me about their investment problems," Madam Sorina said. "But I'm in a conference now. You'll have to make an appointment."

"I have to see you before the market closes," I said. "Money is no object." She told me to come right over.

The investment counselor was a dark-haired, beautiful career woman in her late twenties. She was sitting in the executive suite of a storefront office on West Thirtieth Street, reading *The Wall Street Journal* by candlelight. "Are you Madam Sorina?" I asked, taking out my list of planned purchases.

"No," she said in a thick Mittel-Europa accent. "Madam Sorina had to leave town unexpectedly."

"But I just made an appointment with her to discuss my portfolio."

"I am qualified for this work," she said. "Sorina taught me everything she knows."

"Are you her daughter?"

"No. I bought the business. My name is Madam Marie."

The investment counselor started playing a game that looked like Transylvanian solitaire on her desk, a low tea table next to a couch.

"The cards say you are being followed by a mysterious blond woman," she said, reading three cards. "You are very attractive to women . . ."

"Who told you that?"

"God gave me my psychic powers."

"Look, I didn't come all the way up here from Wall Street to discuss my private life." Since she already had proven her reliability, however, I gave her the big question. "What do you recommend I buy next?"

Her brows knitted in concentration, she played another hand with the cards. It was so quiet in the suite you could hear the market drop. "The cards say," she whispered, "buy government bonds—a sound investment in today's market."

"Will I become rich in the market?" I asked.

Five minutes later, she answered: "The cards say 'maybe.' " I frowned. "The cards never lie," she added. I offered to pay her a little extra for a more bullish prediction about my financial future. "The cards have finished speaking," she said. "Please. Five dollars."

"How would you like to make some really big money?" I said. "I'll give you a bond from my portfolio. You put it inside a chicken and double or triple my investment. Then we'll split seventy–thirty." That was a financial trick many gypsy fortunetellers claim they can perform with their clients' valuables. But Madam Marie refused to handle my securities, because she didn't have a broker's license.

Cheered by the prediction that prosperity might be around the corner, I plunged back into the market, this time giving my business to a Wall Street brokerage house specializing in East European securities. Carl Marks and Company doesn't deal directly with the public, but I managed to get inside with an introduction from Friedrich Engels. A sympathetic Marks executive found many of the must-buy issues on my list at the bottom of the worthless-bond vault. At the end of frantic trading that week, my portfolio contained the following new securities:

RAILROADS: Grand Russian, Trans-Caspian and East-Ural; Trans-Caucasian Railroad 3 percent of 1879; Austro-Hungarian Empire Staats-Eisenbahn-Gesellschaft 3½ percent of 1869; and Budapest Subway 4 percent of 1897.

INDUSTRIALS: Wumag Waggon- und Maschinenbau Aktiengesellschaft Görlitz (East Germany); Galicia-Carpathian Oil Company (Poland); Cuban Cane Products Company Twenty-Year Gold Debentures of 1931; and Guantánamo Sugar Company (common).

GOVERNMENTS: Imperial Russian Government Short-Term War Loan 5½ percent of 1916; Lithuanian Liberty Loan of 1920; and Roumanie Tabac Monopoly 4½ percent of 1937.

MUNICIPALS: City of Odessa Electric Works 4½ percent of 1917; City of Kershon (U.S.S.R.) Sewer Development Authority 4½ percent of 1917; and City of Bucharest 5 percent of 1888.

The prices at which I bought ranged from $1.50 to $3, the most costly issue being Guantánamo Sugar, an especially attractive security for the long haul. If the U.S. planned to destroy the market for Cuban sugar, they would have done it a long time ago by implementing CIA's scheme for bringing Castro to his knees: flooding the world market with surplus synthetic sugar substitutes, thus creating a taste for saccharin.

The next few weeks I was busy managing my portfolio in a businesslike manner. I sent registered letters to each of my companies, announcing the change in ownership of their bonds and stocks. "The previous owners of bond No. 326901," I reported to the chairman of the board of Galicia-Carpathian Oil Company, "claim they have not been receiving annual statements lately. Everybody in New Jersey knows of Galicianas' reputation for honesty, but I suggest you look into this oversight. It will firm up the market for our company's securities."

I also used what little influence I had in Washington to help solve a small problem at Trans-Siberian. I appealed as a U.S. Army veteran to Defense Secretary McNamara that he omit my railroad as a target in any future plan to escalate the Vietnam peace effort. His job was to protect American businessmen's interests abroad, I explained, not to bomb them. Lest Russia's agents in the Pentagon report me to Moscow as another Lord Russell, I sent a carbon copy of my McNamara letter to the Corporate Relations Department of the Ministry of Railroads, at the same time announcing that I would be a candidate for the Trans-Siberian board of directors in the next free election. "I don't want to seem like I'm telling you how to run the railroad," I added, "but what is current management doing to profit from the increasing rate of alcoholism in the Soviet Union? Couldn't we make a few kopecks by adding bar cars to our commuter trains?"

Just because I was now what economists at the Jay Gould School of Finance in Volgograd called a "millionaire"—a Western capitalist whose holdings added up to a million rubles, zlotys, florins, koruny, pesos, lei and Deutsche marks' worth of securities—I didn't rest on my laurels. I soon found myself trying to increase the value of my portfolio by manipulating the market.

I paid a business call to an agency whose primary function, many of its critics had been saying, is to promote capitalism behind the Iron Curtain. The receptionist at Radio Free Europe headquarters on Park Avenue immediately summoned a staff economist as soon as I showed her some of my bonds. The Hungarian émigré studied the pieces in my portfolio for a long while. He mistakenly thought I had come to him for advice. "Sell," he said in broken English.

"But wouldn't it give encouragement to the enslaved peoples behind the Iron Curtain to know that an American industrialist was investing in their future?"

"It would be good news," he said. "The majority of people over there are anti-Communist."

"Well, is there anything in the FCC rules against your plugging some of my securities on one of your big-business shows, preferably during the prime listening time at 2 A.M.? Once the captive peoples heard that I was long in Galicia-Carpathian Oil, the price would go up on the underground Prague Stock Exchange. And be sure to mention that my company still has offshore drilling rights in the Black Sea."

The dollar-fed, revanchist, right-wing émigré

**37**

didn't seem to understand the principle of plugola. So I clipped a coupon from the Galicia-Carpathian bond and handed it to him, murmuring that it was a little something for his trouble. He thanked me politely. "It's nothing," I said, just as politely.

He finally said, "Ahhh, you are talking about buying a commercial. You want to advertise your stocks and bonds."

I took back the coupon and asked to see Radio Free Europe's rate card. In the struggle for markets behind the Iron Curtain, he explained, both Coca-Cola and Pepsi-Cola had already inquired about sponsoring programs to promote the products of their bottling plants in Bulgaria and Hungary. As soon as Radio Free Europe's director decided commercials would not affect the station's nonprofit educational status, he would call me.

What I didn't tell the Hungarian, for fear he would steal my idea, is that I already had decided to pyramid my holdings by using them as a nucleus for a mutual fund. It might be a crime against the state for enslaved peoples to own a share of tsarist business, but I was sure there was no law against owning a share in my mutual fund, which would be sold under the counter to interested small investors. Basically, everybody is a capitalist. For maximum sales appeal in the lands newly discovering the glories of capitalism, I named the fund "The First National Fiduciary Imperialist Trust Syndicate Cartel Pool Combine."

Following is the long exchange of correspondence relevant to setting up a small business in the Soviet Union, which I have sent along to the Securities and Exchange people for their approval.

As First Secretary of the fund, my first official act was to send out feelers to prominent executives who might be interested in aiding this high-minded enterprise. "Congratulations," I wrote to Georgi Malenkov, c/o Personnel Office, the Kremlin. "You have been elected to the board of directors of the First National Fiduciary Imperialist Trust Syndicate Cartel Pool Combine. Once your comrades read about your new post in the world's first mutual coexistence fund—a press release has been mailed to the financial editor of your home-town paper, *Pravda*—you may be asked a few questions. Here are some of the sales points:

"Your mutual fund is an unbalanced open-end investment trust, whose shares will be sold to the peasants at a flexible price. Each according to his need, each according to his ability to pay. Shares will be sold door to door. Is a knock at the door in the middle of the night an effective way to get people in your sales territory away from their TV sets? I look forward to discussing the hydroelectric-plant business with you at the next session of the Party congress or, as Marx meant to call it, the bondholders' meeting."

Similar invitations also went out to other men whose current jobs weren't fully utilizing their proven executive talents: Lazar Kaganovich, Vyacheslav M. Molotov, Nikolai Bulganin, Marshal Georgi Zhukov and Mrs. Nina Khrushchev. As a special bonus incentive, all were invited to be my guests at the annual White

Russian New Year's Ball at the Hotel Astor in New York.

Not wanting anybody to think these men were guilty of plotting with the imperialists, I explained everything in a covering letter to the public relations director of the NKVD at his office in Lubianka Prison, corner of Kirov Street and Dzhershinski Square, Moscow. "Since you've already read my letters," I began, calming the NKVD man's suspicions, "you must be curious to know more about me. I am an ordinary legitimate American speculator currently engaged in rigging the foreign-securities market. In this socially useful work, it is necessary to offer jobs and other valuable rewards in exchange for cooperation. But these are the ordinary costs of doing business under the capitalist system, which your country invented. Are you available to become our mutual fund's public-relations director? Incidentally, where do the commissars keep their yachts?"

All of the Russians accepted the honor; at least, none of them said *nyet*. By not answering, they indicated they wanted to be silent partners. I next made sure the six Russians would always be the minority faction, or Mensheviks, by inviting seven Americans to act as the majority, or Bolsheviks. The list of potential U.S. directors included a few leading Kremlinologists like Oleg and Igor Cassini, Prince Serge Obolensky, Countess Mara and Prince Radziwill. But it was also heavy with prominent anti-Communist military men. Retired generals traditionally welcome top-management positions, so I'm sure General LeMay, General Wainwright and General Walker will be amenable to a telegram reading: "IF ELECTED, WILL YOU SERVE?" If they don't answer, the fund will draft them.

In identical letters to Aleksei Kosygin, Premier, and Leonid Brezhnev, First Secretary of the Party's Central Committee, the fund appealed for the monopoly concession in the hard-to-sell mutual-fund business. Then I asked for some minor changes in the Soviet Union's political structure. "Is there anything you can do about introducing a more peaceful method of conducting your free elections? The Soviet propensity for violent change causes fluctuations in the market, which tends to frighten American speculators and hurt our mutual fund. I know there is no unemployment in Russia, but when you step down because of ill health, would you be interested in a sedentary position as manager of my future estate in Russia?"

I sent a routine note to the procurator general (equivalent to the U.S. Attorney General) at the Ministry of Justice, Moscow: "Please send me copies of all the laws dealing with embezzlement, mail fraud and other economic crimes against the state. I fear my competitors will stop at nothing to drive me out of business. The antifraud laws I have read about in the bourgeois Western press are good—as far as they go. But they seem to be used discriminately against Jews. The laws need stiffening. I plan to urge my representative in the Supreme Soviet—incidentally, who represents the American imperialists?—to demand that the laws be amended to restrain all my competition, regardless of race, creed or religion. In your reply, please give me assurances the First

National Fiduciary Imperialist Trust Syndicate Cartel Pool Combine will not appear on the procurator general's subversive list at some future date."

Once the mutual fund got off the ground, it would obviously have to reinvest in the Russian economy to protect its own interests. A Russian scholar at Columbia University recommended that I contact State Planning Commission Director S. Dimshits. I wanted to write to Comrade Dimshits in his native language, but I knew how sensitive the Russians were about ethnic backgrounds. "If the mutual fund's investments would only affect the petty-cash column in the next Gosplan, landsman," I finally wrote in English, "it wouldn't matter. But the fund is already in railroads, electricity and sewers. We also plan to buy into an electronics firm (one of those manufacturing the surveillance devices that are found in every American Government office), a red-tape factory and a printing plant where dialectical matériels are processed. It would enhance your reputation as a sound economic planner if you did not make any major investments in your next five-year plan until you've checked with your coreligionist.

"P.S. I could even triple the fund's investments in the Soviet economy if you would use your influence at the state bank to help me hustle a loan. The bank still hasn't answered my request for a small-businessman's loan of one million imperial rubles. Can you ring them up and find out the reason for the delay?"

I'm still waiting for his reply.

Finally, however, on January 26, 1967, the Russian government recognized the mutual fund. "In reply to all your letters of 1966," wrote the chief of the consular division, U.S.S.R. Embassy, in Washington, "please be advised that foreign loans, absolutely and without exception, are annulled. So your bonds are completely without value."

Behind the Russians' corporate double talk was the best news investors in Iron Curtain securities had heard in years: Moscow was mouthing the Wall Street line. The future has never looked brighter for the First National Fiduciary Imperialist Trust Syndicate Cartel Pool Combine. Naturally, there are still a few technical difficulties to be ironed out before the fund's strategy will actually inspire confidence. But if you want to get in on the ground floor of a good thing before total peace breaks out, now is the time to buy low.

---

Lest my enemies in television accuse me of ulterior motives in discussing the recent Federal Communications Commission (FCC) decision to seek an eventual ban on TV cigarette advertising, I would like to assure the reader that my interest in the subject is as high-minded as that of any other stockholder in the tobacco industry. My company, R. J. Reynolds of Winston-Salem, spent $48 million in television last year. But I didn't buy into the company to influence Reynolds-sponsored shows more directly than I could have as a critic. I simply wanted to make a killing in the segment of the securities business which might be called the "death-wish market." This is where men profit from the neuroses of others.

*Playing the Death Market*

**43**

The logic behind investing in this area is that the American consumer has proven he will continue to buy harmful products out of psychological needs. I began buying tobacco stock in 1964, a week after the release of the famed Surgeon General's report. The wide publicity given the report, I felt, would help tobacco stocks by making everybody cigarette conscious.

Despite the soundness of my theory, I hedged a little and found two partners with whom I formed a syndicate, called Coso Nostro Investment and Asphalt Paving Company (cable address: The Yellow Hand). Its corporate motto is: "You Always Hurt the One You Love." The Yellow Hand decided to take a position in R. J. Reynolds because their cigarettes, especially Camels, are harsher, definitely harsher. The syndicate went into other promising death-market situations, too: sugar substitutes that are supposed to cause cancer, pesticides, nylon stockings (sales went up after the escapades of the Boston Strangler) and, following the publication of Ralph Nader's book, automobiles. We also sold short on good companies—Gerber products, school textbook publishers, etc. But at this time I only want to discuss The Yellow Hand's tobacco holdings, for they shall be affected by the FCC's decision.

The Yellow Hand's broker, Merrill Lynch, Pierce, Fenner & Smith, recommended that we buy Reynolds at 42⅞ since all tobacco stocks were at rock bottom after the Surgeon General's warning. Within a week, our one share of Reynolds common plunged to 38. Subsequently, the market came to its senses on cigarettes. The inalienable right of every American to smoke himself to death was exercised and a rally occurred. Aided by the kind of government publicity money can't buy, Reynolds went to 40, 42, 45, 48, and then 51½. The only thing that kept our guilt-edged stock from going through the roof was the attitude of management.

Every time investors picked up a copy of *The Wall Street Journal*, there seemed to be a story about some new R. J. Reynolds acquisition: one week a Hawaiian punch company, the next Chinese frozen foods. Investors lost confidence in the cigarette business because of this diversification program, seemingly based on fear. It didn't help either when *The New York Times* reported one morning that a group of cigarette companies had given $10 million to the American Medical Association (AMA) to study the relationship of smoking to disease.

"We're sure you'll be as surprised as we were," The Yellow Hand wrote Reynolds' president, Bowman Gray, "to learn that R. J. Reynolds is one of the tobacco companies participating in this senseless scheme. If we had wanted to cure cancer," the letter went on to explain, "we would have invested in the American Cancer Society. The Surgeon General has already made this study. If we are duplicating it, then the AMA grant is a waste of stockholder's money. If we are merely buying the subsidiary rights to his report, then $10 million is too much to pay. What really makes us nervous is the *Times* report that the money was given to the AMA research project 'without strings attached.' We have never given

**45**

money to the Tobacco Research Council on such terms, and this is not the right time to start setting precedents."

On the basis of past experience with tobacco's top management, The Yellow Hand is convinced that at this very moment Reynolds' officials and their counterparts elsewhere in the industry are probably scheming to find ways to circumvent the expected ban on cigarette commercials on television. Reynolds is inviting a minority stockholder's suit, for The Yellow Hand considers this another blunder. Everybody who watches television already knows cigarettes are bad for them.

The only effective cigarette commercials on the air today are those of the American Cancer Society. The bulk of the television audience, ages five to ten, believes the Cancer Society messages because they sound true. No matter how many times you tell these kids that "You can take Salem out of the country, but you can't take the country out of Salem," it still sounds like a non sequitur. Cigarette commercials have never had much to say; with all the restrictions on copy now, they are more vacuous than ever. The resurrection of the old theme, "I'd walk a mile for a Camel," reveals the desperation of copywriters. The more the ad men try to delude kids, the more they become radicalized. Everyone has heard of young revolutionaries who are refusing to fetch a cigarette for a parent, or going through drawers and throwing out whole cartons. They mean well.

Honesty is the only policy for the cigarette companies. To compete with the American Cancer Society, cigarette commercials should simply say: "Smoke Brand X—they satisfy your death wish."

What will happen if the tobacco industry is forced to pull out of television? First, the American Cancer Society commercials will disappear, since the equal-time requirement will no longer apply. Then, it will be business as usual for the cigarette companies.

R. J. Reynolds could have performed a real public service by using its $48 million advertising budget to save a great American institution, the *Saturday Evening Post*. The literary reviews, poetry, and the scholarly quarterlies could still profit from Reynolds' largesse.

We are going to miss some television cigarette commercials. My favorite was the spot for Virginia Slims, a cigarette designed exclusively for women. A fellow in *Variety* claimed they would be followed by Minnesota Fats (for hustlers) and New York Broads. The good commercials will grow in stature over the years, much the way *Omnibus* has.

The Yellow Hand, of course, wasn't the only group affected by the FCC decision. It must have stunned Republicans that one of the initial concrete acts of the Nixon Administration was the meddling of a regulatory agency in the internal affairs of a private enterprise like broadcasting. The commissioners' broadened interpretation of FCC powers may kill television as we know it.

If it is injurious for people to watch cigarette commercials, as the FCC seems to have concluded four years after the Surgeon General's report, it is even more dangerous for the public to watch actors smoking. Many people feel like smoking only when they see somebody else lighting up. It's like watching sex or violence. On the evening of February 16, I counted thirty-seven actors smoking on television, usually during moments of extreme dramatic tension.

These free commercials are so commonplace on TV that after years of watching private eyes and Westerns, the average person, before or after killing somebody, automatically reaches for the weed. We naturally identify with the glamorous image of the heroes and villains. Thus, allowing so much smoking on television is comparable to the cruelty of showing a picture of chocolate cake to somebody on a diet.

The American Cancer Society school of realism tells the viewer what actually happens to people who smoke. It is in realism, too, that the FCC will find the solution to this dilemma. There are great romantic figures who in real life don't turn to cigarettes in moments of tension. It would be gratifying to my image if television heroes were shown biting their nails to relieve tension. Real people also chew pencils, or scratch their hair. Sometimes they get cramps or raid the refrigerator.

But a "No Smoking" rule would make it hard for young actors to establish a name for themselves. The best acting in many a TV series today occurs during the ritual of smoking. To cite a classic example from the world of film, Robert Mitchum could never have become a star in a medium which did not allow an actor to blow smoke from his flared nostrils.

In time, I suppose, acting schools will teach

young actors how to bite their nails, or whatever, and save television drama. But the situation is hopeless in educational TV. The number of people with the nerves of steel who can appear on a discussion show without smoking is limited.

---

After fourteen years of thorough study by the nation's smartest military minds, the Pentagon decided the best way to stop Communist Chinese aggression was to build an ABM site in Tenafly, New Jersey—a wealthy residential area on the outskirts of New York City, only 4.7 miles from my house in Leonia, New Jersey (pop. 9,000).

Some people said the ABM was an unmitigated disaster for Bergen County. Others said we couldn't live without it. Both sides were persuasive. At the time I had a big investment in my old Leonia home. Property values would diminish overnight in case of nuclear attack. Out of self-interest, I decided to do something about protecting my investment.

I wrote directly to Secretary of Defense Melvin Laird urging him to abandon building the ABM site in Tenafly because that borough has continually agitated against the war in Vietnam, and been for "peace." "Hopefully your decision giving it to them was a punitive measure. It seems to me a better idea to give ABMs to towns which deserve them."

Leonia (founded 1667) is as much a residential area as Tenafly, I explained, but with the advantage that it is solidly Republican. On the basis of eight years' residence, I believed it

*The L. Mendel Rivers Experimental Missile Base*

**49**

worthy of a federal plum like a missile site.

Leonians are brave, I pointed out, because they have not been frightened by Tenafly's "Mayor's Missile Committee" and "Citizens Against the Tenafly Antiballistic-Missile Site," who told us that Tenafly may be in the BLAST area of a nuclear attack, but Leonia is in the FIRE area. We'd sooner be in the BLAST area than the FIRE area; we've got wood houses. (I'm a BODY-BURN man myself.)

"Leonia also has a vigorous American Legion post which can be counted on to support an ABM missile site," I assured the Secretary of Defense, "because, as you have said, 'it is a contribution to world peace.' The sentiment here, I'm happy to say, is better dead than red (or yellow)."

The borough, the letter added, is vulnerable to attack and is without any means to retaliate.

Our town is located only one mile and a half from the George Washington Bridge. Bridges are always important targets, as demonstrated by our bombing policy in Vietnam. The Chinese high command will undoubtedly want to bomb the George Washington Bridge in order to protect the civilian population in the Metropolitan New York area from harm.

My reasoning about the danger went like this:

1) The Chinese ballistic-missile system is far from accurate (God knows how I knew this).

2) Thus, when the Chinese attempted to destroy our antiballistic-missile system, they would aim for where they are, and hit somewhere else.

3) As a veteran and a graduate of Brooklyn Technical High School, I ascertained that the

safest place to be during the attack by the Chinese would be the place where the Chinese were aiming at.

4) I.e., if they aimed at Leonia's missile station, the chances are good they would hit Tenafly or Teaneck. The worst thing that could happen to us in the coming Sino-American War was to have nothing in town that would take the scrutable Oriental military mind off that damn George Washington Bridge.

To prove that my letter wasn't just another one of those flag-waving gestures, I patriotically offered my family's little white house and yard in Leonia for consideration as an alternative to the site then under attack by the SDS-type crazies in Tenafly. "Should you have already picked out the ghetto area in Englewood for the new ABM site," my letter said, "please consider this a formal application for the anti-antiballistic-missile missile site. P.S. Can you please send me the building specifications for the so-called 'thin' missile, so I can get some idea whether it will fit in my back yard.'"

The only dimensions I had read about in the papers was ABM silos were dug one hundred feet deep in the ground. My land more than met that specification.

I sent a carbon copy of my confidential letter to the Pentagon to our local paper to express my belief in freedom of the press. A reporter was at my house within hours.

"I think Laird would be a fool to pass up acquiring a parcel of land in such a vital strategic area," I explained. "But you know government: Laird probably assigned the Kitman matter to a task force and that'll be the last Leonia will ever hear about it."

I explained I planned to hire a powerful lobbyist to sit in Washington, preferably in Laird's office, and push the project—somebody like Curtis LeMay. This was a matter of life and death to Leonia.

The Pentagon was so lax in making these ABM decisions, I apologized for Laird, because they know the Chinese are not going to bomb Washington, in line with our Hanoi principle. There is probably a tacit agreement amongst the world's politicians not to bomb each other's capitals. Those of us who live near the bridges don't have that assurance.

I explained that I intended to finance the project, which included having the Nixon administration designate Leonia as temporary capital of the United States in case of attack, through a local door-to-door campaign for contributions. Boy Scouts may collect the money for the Leonia War Chest so they can qualify for public-health merit badges.

"What if the Pentagon turns you down?" asked the reporter at the exclusive interview.

My plan was designed to self-destruct in four weeks, I explained. I couldn't sit around all spring on tenterhooks. My lawn needed work.

The good news that a Leonia man had offered to save the ABM program in Bergen County broke on the front page of the *Bergen Record* on a leisurely Sunday in February like a bombshell. "Mayor Cassius Daly said he will take the matter up with the Borough Council at their Monday meeting," the Hackensack paper reported. " 'I'm not interested in anything that would take ratables away from the borough,' the Mayor said. 'It's not sound thinking at all. Kitman lives on Crescent Avenue—that's a densely populated area.' "

Commander Livingston C. Douglas of American Legion Post #1 (Leonia), the paper reported, "lauded Kitman's generosity, but said the project required more study. 'I don't even know what the thing looks like,' Douglas said. 'If he lives on a hill, they'll have to go through a lot of trap rock to put in a silo.' "

"He responds with a combination of information and fatalism to questions about accidental detonation," the story said about my answer to the problem of the ABM's reliability: "Naturally, I'm concerned, but I've heard the safest place to be with these things is next to the missilemen pushing the buttons. Anyhow if you're going to worry about accidents, why you could get hit by a car!"

What I was trying to say is that it didn't matter much whether the ABM worked or not. The people of Leonia would be able to sleep better at night, even if the ABM turned out to be only a security symbol. Rising out of my garden, it would also be a phallic symbol which might improve my chances of being invited to join the *dolce vita* set in town. Besides if it didn't work—as Jerome Wiesner, provost of MIT, pointed out in the Senate hearings later on—we could always send it back to the manufacturer.

"Lest anyone think him a Pollyanna," the newspaper story ended, "Kitman says although he will donate his land, he will insist on the PX and noncommissioned-officers' club concessions. He hotly denies his proposal is a ploy to bring a ratable into the community, but he ad-

**53**

mits that there is a Chinese restaurant in Leonia where the spies could eat.

"Secretary Laird has not yet responded to Kitman's letter. A secretary in the Department of Defense said that Laird was not in and she did not know where to reach him."

A lot of people mistakenly called me, instead of Laird, that day. I gave the callers the Pentagon's phone number, with assurances that the matter was out of my hands. The Department of Defense, in its wisdom, decided where the missiles go, not an average citizen.

Support for my proposal flowed in from all over Bergen County. "If there is anything we can do," went a typical expression from a Tenafly man, "to help put Leonia in the blast area, feel free to call on us."

At the Borough Council meeting the next night, "the ABM site got no support from borough officials," according to the weekly *Leonia Life*. "The danger that the elementary-school pupils might set off the missile accidentally while walking to and from school was cited by Councilman Zealy Gerber in opposing Kitman's plan. Gerber also said that property in the borough would be devalued, except for those who rented rooms to spies. Insurance premiums would also rise."

Mayor Daly, a solidly conservative Republican who is vice president for mortgages in a local bank, wrote a poem of protest, which he delivered as the town's official position:

> *In turning Kitman down*
> *We won't lose face.*
> *So, please, for Leonia*
> *No missile base.*

What struck me about the hidden message in

that awful example of *bank verse* was that the Mayor's position on the missile base seemed identical with that of the Women's Strike for Peace, SANE, and other left-leaning groups. Until then, I hadn't known that the bank's mortgage department was led by a peacenik.

Some gossips said the reason I stayed away from the Borough Council meeting that night was my fear of facing my neighbors. The truth is Mayor Daly and the councilmen had no business meddling in international affairs that way. What war college or general staff school had these members of the intellectual establishment attended? Our municipal government was having enough trouble coping with sewers and air pollution from the Chinese restaurant without getting in over their heads on defense problems. It sounded as if Mayor Daly was using the ABM as a stepping stone for national office.

I was above the battle. "Nevertheless, should the Democratic Party wish to sponsor a forum on Leonia's missile gap," I wrote to the chairman of a local opposition group, "I will be glad to participate as a spokesman for the hard-liners on defending the town against Red China. Mayor Daly could speak for those who are soft on this issue. The mayor can choose his weapons in the debate—verse or prose."

With his nose for a big story, that muckraking Hackensack reporter got on the phone the next day to find out what Secretary Laird was planning to do about Leonia. After an hour he finally was bucked down to Colonel Roger Bankson, Director of Information at the Pentagon. A search of the files was instituted while the reporter hung on. It was then that the Pentagon announced officially that my letter had been lost.

As a student of military information policies, the reporter was suspicious. It sounded to him like the standard U-2 ploy, or telling the truth.

"It occured to me last night, while I was trying to fall asleep after reading your horrifying testimony before Congress on the dangers of the growing Red Chinese missile program, that the reason for the delay in your acceptance of my land may be that the letter has been misplaced," I wrote to Secretary Laird the next morning. "I am enclosing six carbon copies of the original. Please let me know if you need any more.

"These decisions take time, I realize. But I wonder if in the interim you would be good enough to send me a letter which made the following points:

1. The Secretary has referred your letter to me for reply.
2. Thank you for bringing this matter to our attention. You can be sure it will receive our careful consideration.
3. Secretary Laird is currently reviewing our total defense posture, with special emphasis on the ABM program.
4. Thank you for your interest in national security.
   Sincerely yours,
   (Mrs.) Rosetta Blotz
   Administrative Assistant
   Office of Crank Mail/OSD

"You can put it in your own language. A message like this would be very helpful to me in preparing the folks for the army trucks which may someday come rolling into town at 0600 hours.

"I have a group of men—veterans like myself—who are ready to man the mimeograph machines. Our group is called the Just-a-Min-utemen. All we need is a definite maybe from your office, and we'll start selling this thing to the community."

The reply from the Office of the Chief of Staff was very significant. Colonel B. A. Griffin, Assistant Sentinel System Manager, didn't say, "You must be kidding about your *back yard.*" "With regard to your offer of land," Gen. Starbird's assistant *himself* wrote, in part, "it . . . will receive full consideration prior to any decision being made. Your interest in the Sentinel system is appreciated."

The Just-a-Minutemen were very encouraged by this signal from the Pentagon. Before we got started on this thing, Leonia wasn't being considered by the master planners at all. Now we were being considered, along with other sites. We certainly had come a long way in a short time. It shows how responsive our Pentagon was to the people. As they say in Washington, the ball was in their court.

It was decided to name the missile base after the person who would have done the most to give it to Leonia. In a democratic fashion, the names of the 435 Congressmen were thrown into a brass hat. That's how it came to be known as the L. Mendel Rivers Experimental Missile Center. The powerful chairman of the House Armed Services Committee would get an invitation to cut the red tape opening the site for active duty. A case of bourbon was stockpiled for that happy day.

Meanwhile, I went ahead and strung up some barbed wire in front of my lawn. A sign

read: KEEP OUT . . . RESTRICTED AREA . . . TRES-
PASSERS WILL BE ELECTROCUTED . . . NO RED CHI-
NESE ALLOWED . . . and so forth. It was just a
neighborly reminder that the government was
currently considering this area as an ABM missile site, in case they had missed the story in
the Bergen County press:

PENTAGON RECEIVES
PLANS FOR ROCKETS
Leonia.—Marvin Kitman's plan for relocation of a
proposed antiballistic-missile site from Tenafly to
the borough has been received and filed by the
Pentagon . . .

Ex-Mayor John Stencken of Leonia said at
the next week's council meeting that the borough should put my property in escrow, as a
precaution in the case the Pentagon decided to
proceed. The liberal-academic complex in town
formed the Leonia Committee for Prevention
of the Establishment of Antiballistic Missiles
on Crescent Avenue, from Broad Avenue, East,
Including Maple and Prospect Streets." The ad
hoc committee's letters to the editor in the
local papers were a new low in yellow journalism, much worse than anything in the mainland Chinese press about me. The gist was
that I was trying to get even with my neighbors with the L. Mendel Rivers Experimental
Missile Center.

I next urged the director of the Adult Education Center of Leonia to give a course in
Pentagonese. The curriculum would cover such
important words of tomorrow as *implemental
realization* (def., a fact), *rocket propellant personnel neutralizers* (def., portable showers using ordinary water built for use of missilemen
who accidentally spill rocket fuel on them-

58

selves) and *reconfiguration* (def., how to figure out a plausible new reason for going ahead with a multibillion-dollar boondoggle). That was one word I hoped we'd never have to use in Leonia.

At the same time, we were enlisting citizens in a unique type of antiprotest protest. Should Washington be shortsighted enough to turn down the Leonia self-defense program, we were recommending a mass *overpayment* of taxes on April 15. This would confound the government computers, require untold hours of refunding labor and throw the national budget completely out of kilter. By having everyone overpay on income taxes, we could easily demonstrate the essential patriotism of the movement.

Naturally I was in no position to predict whether the L. Mendel Rivers Experimental Missile Center would ever get off the Pentagon's drawing boards, but I was urging all of my friends who didn't love the ABM to look for houses in Tenafly, as it had been rumored that I had been doing.

With the Maoist-liberal-mothers-anti-ABM forces in a state of confusion and disarray in Leonia, I was disturbed to read in the papers one day in March that President Nixon seemingly was taking the lunatic fringe's uninformed views seriously. He was reviewing the entire ABM problem with the Secretary of Defense at Key Biscayne, according to newspaper reports, with an eye to reconfiguring. While the President met with Laird, I met with Herman Kahn at the Hudson Institute.

Some of my neighbors said I had been getting a little uppity after the Pentagon said it

**59**

was considering giving me my missile. But it was logical that I should turn to Kahn for advice on Leonia's defense posture. Kahn is known as an expert on fighting World War III. His real expertise is in getting government contracts. We could use all of his skill as a military strategist-economist-mathematician-sociologist-geneticist-political-scientist-patriot-and-government-influence man. He also thinks of himself as a do-gooder. Dr. Kahn agreed to give me thirty minutes of his time, I guess, because Leonia's defense problems were small.

I am still not sure that I understood everything he said during the visit to his famed think tank in the woods at Croton-on-Hudson, New York. He is a very bright man, a fat Groucho Marx with a 400 I.Q., and an exceptionally fast talker. I have a mind like a steel sieve, which tends to go blank when I try to think about the unthinkable.

There was a temptation to start off with a theoretical question like, "Why is it that ABMs around missile sites maintain a strategy of deterrence, while ABMs around cities prepare for a first-strike capability?" But that might consume the whole thirty minutes. I plunged right into the technical difficulties in my missile plan: "If they accept my land, should I ask for a ninety-nine-year lease or a couple of destroyers?"

The 280-pound (approx.) man looked at me fiercely from behind mountains of secret papers scattered over his desk, and spoke in a machinegunlike staccato voice: "I recognize that you are being satirical in some of your points. . . . Satire is an ancient honorable system of thought. . . . The main thrust of the argument is no less valid because of the way it is couched. . . . Your Leonia is in danger from the Chinese. . . . I am in favor of getting a nuclear deterrent for Leonia, as a matter of principle. . . . It is only unfortunate that Leonia happens to be 'the bedroom of Columbia.' . . . You have the largest per-capita number of Columbia faculty in the nation. . . . But I am willing to overlook Columbia's virulent attacks on the Hudson Institute staff. . . ."

Before we went any further, I asked him how much he charged for thinking. "Our fees range from two hundred thousand dollars down to zero," he explained, "depending on how interested our consultants are in the individual project." I told Kahn Leonia could raise the latter figure, and we proceeded.

"As our consultant, would the best first step be for you to call Laird's office? Or would you want to analyze this test boring from the site?"

"I'm not going to serve as Leonia's lobbyist," he shouted. "Because the President is going to stab you in the back. In three days he's going to announce his decision to cut back the ABM Sentinel system. I'm with you 100 percent in the fight. But I'm allergic to going down with my flags flying—even if it is only a temporary defeat. In the long run I'm convinced the government will have to go through with the original Sentinel plan for full deployment."

I protested that the Pentagon had said that we needed the ABM Sentinel system against the Chinese *now*, if we were to preserve the American way of life. The Defense Department knows what it is doing.

The man whose writings have awakened many Americans to the horrors of a thermonuclear war recently explained to *The New York Times* why he was the most hated intellectual in the nation: "I'm the messenger who brings bad news. In the olden days anyone who brought bad news was punished and tortured. Things have not really changed today." Kahn lived up to his reputation.

"You're insane!" he screeched at me, sputtering and throwing his arms wildly over his head. "They do *not* know what they are doing!" He whipped out a sheaf of papers from under the pile. "Look at Volume 25 of *Nuclear Arms Control Issues*, and Chart Collection No. 3, *Policy Issues Facing the New Administration*." They were classified, so he gave me a chance to look at the documents and charts only briefly, before pulling them out of my hands. "The average age of the generals in the Chiefs of Staff's Office—fifty-six." His voice was cold as liquid hydrogen. "Far too old to adapt to the swift pace of modern technology. Do you know the secret of what makes this country great?"

"No," I confessed.

"The only thing that saves this country from extinction is the average age of the Russian general staff. Look at this." He passed another secret chart under my nose. "Sixty-three. Poor Khrushchev. In order to get them to stop building battleships, he had to shoot the admirals."

I was struck dumb by these secret revelations, but Dr. Kahn hardly seemed to notice. "I will assign Leonia's problems to my second in command. Dr. Brennan still believes in the original ABM plan and loves a good losing fight."

Fortunately, I had been warned not to believe a word Kahn said. So by the time I escaped from the think tank and drove back across the George Washington Bridge to New Jersey, my old optimism about surviving a nuclear war returned. I drew up my will, and settled down to await the arrival of either the American or the Chinese missile, which Secretary Laird was still telling the press was to be expected momentarily. A few days later, President Nixon announced his decision to pull the missiles out of the Leonia-Tenafly complex, as well as the thirteen other carefully picked suburban sites. "Not in my back yard; not in your back yard; not in anybody's back yard," he seemed to be saying. This was a victory for us, in the sense of U.S. victories in Vietnam. New Jersey's Senators Case and Williams had opposed the ABM program. The President had been put on notice that New Jersey's representatives could not live with any defense plan which ignored Leonia. Nevertheless, the decision produced consternation at the proposed L. Mendel Rivers Experimental Missile Center.

At issue in the great national debate that followed was whether the cities with all their problems were worth saving. The President's latest position—the so-called Safeguard system —was that the country could afford to save only the rural Midwestern areas. Why he suddenly decided to abandon the cities to the Red Chinese is a top secret. My guess was that it had something to do with politics. The Nixon strategy called for saving the Republican countryside and sacrificing the Democratic urban East to the yellow hordes. That's what

Republicans in the small towns bordering the big cities would call false economy.

It might well have triggered an urban-rural migration. The only thing that prevented widespread defection to the Red Chinese was the realization that the President had made a snap decision. He had been out of town a lot during the early weeks of his administration, and everybody was demanding that he say something firm. So he took the middle road. Fortunately, he left open his options to change his mind. The first crisis—such as a drop in profits in the military-industrial complex—will bring the sound Sentinel system in an expanded and improved version.

What Leonia needed, it seemed to me in the most critical hour of the 303-year history of the borough, was a reliable third-strike capability. It was the last of the ninth with two out and President Nixon at bat, and we had no deterrent. If the Pentagon couldn't give satisfaction, I would have to find another way to defend the territorial integrity of my home from a sneak Chinese Communist attack. On the theory that the best defense is an offense, I decided to build the L. Mendel Rivers missile base myself, using old-fashioned New Jersey ingenuity.

First, we founded the East Hudson Institute, which began shopping around for ultimate deterrents. Dr. Brennan of the original Hudson Institute had one in his files that he was willing to let go as a contribution to Leonia's Save-Our-Town program. The basic idea of what he termed "the turnabout technique" was quite simple. It called for placing a large number of rigidly fixed rocket engines in a band around the earth's equator. Then, when an incoming enemy warhead is detected, these rocket engines are all turned on simultaneously. The resulting thrust would turn the globe 180 degrees between the time of detection and the time of impact. The missile would therefore land on the enemy's own territory, and contribute to his own destruction.

Dr. Brennan told me, "The genius of the plan is that all the mathematics checks out. The only problem with it is that the cost of the program will bankrupt the country." Senator Symington said the same thing about the Nixon administration's ABM program, so it couldn't be any worse.

After studying the four pages of calculations, I wrote to Leonia's first defense consultant, "Your proposal amused me. You give the formula for finding the moment of inertia (I) for a uniform sphere of the earth's mass, 'I = $(2/5)$ mR$^2$ = $9.75 \times 10^{44}$ gram = cm.$^2$.' This must be your idea of a joke. You know that the earth is not a uniform sphere of mass. But that's not nearly as flagrant as your omitting the Coriolis effect in your calculations, presumably because it is as imaginary as centrifugal force. Your numbers, such as 'rockets needed = $10^{19}$,' may seem large to the average layman, but they are not so large when delving into the number of atoms in the universe ($10^{74}$). Don't try to fool me with your scientific notations.

"By the way, my son's science teacher, Mark Schubin, told him what the Hudson Institute does. He therefore requests that you pay him for the above critique of your theory."

After firing the Hudson Instiute as consul-

**65**

tants for poor thinking, we hired a German scientist, one of the physics professors at Stevens Institute in Hoboken, the closest thing we have to an MIT in New Jersey. This master stroke paid off immediately. "Since deterrence is such a wonderful policy," he wrote, "I thought that you might be able to improve and humanize the policy by being the first on your block to produce a basement H-bomb (providing it doesn't conflict with zoning regulations in Leonia)." He included a paper from the German journal *Zeitschrift für Natürforschung* by H. Opower and W. Press, who were working on a similar project at the Technische Hochschule in Munich. The only difficult thing about the personal Doomsday Machine was building a large enough laser to trigger the ultimate guarantor of universal peace. "Perhaps the Ford Foundation would provide the funds to encourage the growth of science in the suburbs," suggested my German scientist.

It turned out there was nothing on the statute books against building H-bombs in the basement of one-family houses. While one of the more mechanically minded Just-a-Minute-men tinkered in the basement, I got to worrying. Was one H-bomb enough of a deterrent? We might feel more secure if everybody in Leonia was building an H-bomb, but stockpiling hasn't worked for the country, and it wasn't working for me. Fortunately, New Jersey technology was able to produce the ultimate safe deterrent.

By the time you read this, if the Pentagon was right about the imminence of danger from the Red Chinese, you will know whether private enterprise saved Leonia from nuclear attack. If by some unexpected combination of events—most scientists think there is no solution to the problem—it does work, the story of this miracle will have been told many times. All I can do now is give you the scenario, as worked out by the town's scientific advisers at the East Hudson Institute.

1) Leonia will become the nation's first town-state, severing ties with the central government on the strict constitutional grounds that Washington failed to provide for the common defense and domestic tranquillity (Article I, Section 8).

2) As a further vote of no confidence in the Pentagon, everybody will sell his U.S. defense bonds to help finance the new town-state's arms program.

3) Since our private resources will be inadequate, as every other non-Communist state has found, we will next apply for military aid from the United States Government. Should there be any delay in Washington, the request can be expedited by inviting the Russians to send us the fifty-four Communists from the Dominican Republic who goaded President Johnson into action a few years back. They can move into the houses abandoned by the Mayor and the councilmen.

4) To guarantee our neutrality in the East-West struggle, at the same time we will invite Moscow to participate in underwriting Leonia's self-defense program. While we are farther from Washington than Cuba is from Miami, they might still be interested.

5) Because of our past close ties with Washington, and our common roots, at the same time we will propose to a mutual-defense non-

aggression treaty with the United States. We wouldn't want any of these other moves to be misinterpreted as saber rattling.

6) Meanwhile, Leonia's Department of Defense will be hiring a friend of New Jersey, Buckminster Fuller, to design the ultimate deterrent. Leonia is only 3.2 square miles in area, and it shouldn't be any problem for this genius to build a geodesic structure over the town— made out of unbreakable plastic.

7) Then the Russians, our allies in the struggle against the Red Chinese, will be invited to throw one of their Galoshes at our ABM site to prove that it will work.

8) If science is wrong, at least we'll know once and for all.

# PART TWO

# CULTURAL TRENDS

## THE NORTHERN NEW JERSEY SCHOOL OF LITERARY CRITICISM

A question I am often asked as a critic is have I read any good books lately. The one I have been recommending this season is *Who's Who in America*.

The 1968–69 edition tends to drag a little when read from the beginning. So I usually suggest people start with the most interesting part, page 1,220, which includes this passage for the first time in the seventy-year publishing history of *Who's Who*:

*Sp. cons. subcom. legislative oversight U.S. Ho. of Reps., et al*

> KITMAN, Marvin, journalist; b. Pitts., Nov. 24, 1929; s. Myer and Rose (Kaufman) K.; B.A., City Coll. N.Y., 1953; m. Carol Sibushnick, Oct. 28, 1951; children—Jamie Lincoln, Suzy, Andrea Jordana. Columnist, Armstrong Daily, N.Y.C., 1956-66; cons. Al Capp Enterprises, 1961-63; staff writer Sat. Eve. Post, 1965-66; news-mng. editor Monocle mag., N.Y.C., 1963——; TV critic New Leader mag., N.Y.C., 1967——; asst. to treas.

Monocle Periodicals, 1965——; bd. dirs., 1966——; lectr. colls. and univs., 1963——; humorist-in-residence Solow/Wexton, Inc., N.Y.C., 1966——. Mem. Leonia (N.J.) Pub. Library, 1961——. Republican candidate for presdl. nomination, 1964. Served with AUS, 1953-55. Author: The Number-One Best Seller, 1966; (pseudonym William Randolph Hirsch with Robert Lingeman) The RCAF (Red Chinese Air Force) Exercise, Diet and Sex Book, 1967; also articles, book revs. Office: Monocle Mag., 80 Fifth Av., N.Y.C.

I found this page interesting; as a matter of fact, I read it twice. As Byron said in *Childe Harold*: "History, with all her volumes vast,/ Hath but *one* page."

Actually Volume 35 of the biennial "biographical dictionary of notable living men and women" contains 2,563 pages, a distinct improvement over Volume 34, which had but 2,472 pages. As a result, there is more to read in the new edition: 66,000 true stories of the great, compared to only 61,967 in the last version. And it is more timely.

Still, few people seem to be following my recommendation.

In the old days, before I made it, everybody used to read *Who's Who*. Herbert Hoover took the big red book to bed with him every night. He read it, his biographers explain, for entertainment as well as education.

That's about what I expected to get out of *Who's Who* during the three months or so it took me to read the book through from Edwin Garfield Aabye, the Indiana "electric utility exec.," to Antoni Zygmund, the "prof. mathematics U. Chicago." Or was it Carvel G. Zwingle, the "trucking exec." in California?

The only things I could find that might possibly be responsible for the decline in the readership of *Who's Who* today are the book's style and content.

"A well-written life," Thomas Carlyle once observed, "is almost as rare as a well-spent one." Nevertheless the *Who's Who* style is so distinctive—"Sp. cons. subcom. legislative oversight U. S. Ho. of Reps., 1959," they wrote of the formative years in the life of Richard Naradof Goodwin, an "ex-govt. ofcl." on page 859—my curiosity as a student of bad writing was aroused.

In the course of a recent fact-finding trip to the editorial rooms of *Who's Who* in Chicago, I found that the odd style was developed by the book's founding father, Albert Nelson Marquis, in the late 1890s. At the time Marquis was also putting together what was in effect Chicago's telephone directory. Perhaps the one explains the influence of the other, in both literary and typographical style.

There are no by-lines in *Who's Who*, as in the *Encyclopaedia Britannica*. But I managed to trace down the authorship of the 66,000 Biographies, or "sketches," to 25 free-lances. Mostly, the sketch writers are the wives of Chicago-area college professors. "I can use anybody," explained the editor in charge of the *Who's Who* creative writing department, "except professional writers. They can't buckle down to the requirements of our style."

Should anybody be aspiring to a career as a *Who's Who* writer, the secret of the style is not that hard to discover. You have to learn how to write about the life of a painter like Andy Wyeth, on page 2,408, in such a way as to give the reader a very good idea that the man is an artist of some importance, without revealing that his art is any different from that of Andy Warhol, written up on page 2,283.

Not that I would recommend it as a career. For a relatively simple life, like author Irving Wallace's on page 2,772, sketch writers are paid 35 cents. For boiling down the life of a man of greater achievements, such as Grayson Louis Kirk, the "univ. pres." on page 1,216, they have the option of charging the *Who's Who* management for double time.

I know this must make the publishers, Marquis-Who's Who, Inc., sound like the Triangle Shirtwaist Company of the publishing world. But once the mini-Catherine Drinker Bowens get the knack the good ones can sum up as many as ten lives an hour. For the sketch writer who did the piece about Marshall McLuhan, the "communications specialist" on page 2,505, there also must have been a sense of real achievement. Her biography was clearer than anything the great communicator ever wrote.

The hack writing in *Who's Who* is not nearly as important a shortcoming as the book's content, which is basically all facts. It might even be assumed that *Who's Who* is so widely unread because of this obsession with facts.

This notion flies in the face of contemporary literary trends. Whole novels these days are being written about facts. There are the pure facts, as in Truman Capote's *In Cold Blood* and William Styron's *The Confessions of Nat Turner*. And there is an even greater appetite for the impure facts as in Jacqueline Susann's *The Love Machine* and David Slavitt's *The Exhibitionist*. The difference between *Who's Who* and these other collections of facts is the difference between literary style and the amassing of facts which just seem to lie there.

The editors of *Who's Who* go to great pains gathering information that is usually allowed to go ungathered, ranging from my wife's maiden name to the fact that G. David Schine in his two years of military service rose to the rank of private. "A real old hand," I was told at Who's Who, "gets to know precisely what goes in the book and what stays out."

This is not to say that there isn't some useful information in *Who's Who*. I learned, for example, that William Shawn's home address is 1150 Fifth Avenue, a better place for a writer to send the *New Yorker* editor manuscripts that require his undivided attention.

But there is much in it that is neither useful nor interesting. I haven't been able to sleep at night since learning that "ret. air force officer" Curtis E. LeMay was a holder of the Russian Order of the Patriotic War at the same time he served as "cmdr.-in-chief Strategic Air Command."

At least *Who's Who* seems to work as solid journalism—until you start asking where *Who's Who* gets its facts. Since Marquis began the practice, the editors have been asking the notables to supply their own biographical material. The rationale is not that it's cheaper, but that nobody knows himself better. This is tantamount to Dun & Bradstreet asking its notables for an estimate of what they're worth.

The average autobiographical questionnaire returned to *Who's Who* by the biographee resembles an FBI file in one way: it is filled with candid information, much of which is true. Outright lies are rarely printed in the pages of *Who's Who*, but not that rarely—in the entry displayed above a man known to most as Richard Lingeman is renamed Robert.

A top adviser in the Eisenhower administration, for example, exaggerated the number of his degrees. (He didn't have any.) Poets have used some license in claiming other poets' work. Historian Henry Adams became younger with each succeeding edition of *Who's Who*, until he was younger than his younger brother. Even such a paragon as Senator Joseph McCarthy falsified his age. So did Secretary of the Treasury Andrew Mellon and countless women.

At the other extreme are the people who tell us more than we should know about their private life. Lady Bird Johnson ("b. Dec. 22, 1912") is listed as "owner, operator radio-TV sta., KTBC, Austin, Tex. 1942—." I thought I had read in the papers that the Johnson family had divested themselves of their broadcast interests, so there would be no conflict in White House dealings with the FCC.

Grayson Kirk's life story includes the information that he is currently "director of Mobil Oil Co., IBM Corp., Nation-Wide Securities Co., Dividend Shares Inc., Consol. Edison Co. N.Y., Inc.; trustee Greenwich Savs. Bank . . ." With academic qualifications like those, he should have no trouble getting another job.

The inherent weakness in the *Who's Who* approach to biography is that it allows the informants to interpret the significance of their own facts. J. Edgar Hoover, who describes his profession as "dir. FBI," makes full disclosure of his many accomplishments, including his twenty-one degrees from such institutions as Kalamazoo College (D.Sc., 1937) and U. of South (D.C.L., 1941). The only other thing he seems to leave out of his sketch is the little-known fact (according to usually reliable information supplied by this writer to *The New Leader*) that he personally edits the scripts of the television show *The FBI*. But an equally important man like Richard McGarrah Helms modestly lists himself in the pages of *Who's*

*Who* as a "govt. ofcl." You have to be a student of "govt. ofcls." or a counterspy to know that Helms is really the director of the Central Intelligence Agency.

This isn't a case of false modesty. For Helms does note his job briefly: "With CIA, 1947—." Other employees of CIA, such as Jay Lovestone, the "dir. of internat. affairs AFL-CIO," completely omit this important chapter in their lives.

What seems to have happened at *Who's Who* is that its method of fact collecting has taken over its purpose, which should be to inspire the American people. I knew the book wasn't performing adequately in this area either the night I reached page 1,738, which features the biography of Norman Podhoretz. I had half-expected to find a brief note: "MADE IT. For further details, see my book on the subject." His sixteen-line sketch—only one line longer than the man ahead of him alphabetically, Nikolai V. Podgorny, President of the U.S.S.R. —gave all the basic facts contained in his 360-page autobiography, a digesting triumph. But his *Who's Who* life seemed no more inspiring than that of another fan-magazine editor on the same page, Jack Jerry Podell.

So it is not surprising that even the editors of *Who's Who* can't stand reading their finished product through from A to Z at the end of the two years it takes to get the facts and manipulate them. It's such a major achievement, I heard the editors still talking about the time a woman employee named Betty did it several years ago.

There is nothing wrong with *Who's Who* that rewriting the sixty-six thousand biographies wouldn't help. In the meanwhile, it seems to me that the book could be improved as literature simply by printing more of the material submitted by some of the world's best writers. Irving Wallace earns a million dollars or so for an outline not much longer than his autobiographical questionnaire. I had the rare privilege of reading poet Allen Ginsberg's original material, and I must say the parts the editors left out were more engrossing. The *Who's Who* version on page 836 contains this rather dry line: "Poetry readings Columbia, Harvard, Yale."

But Ginsberg actually went on at some length about this subject, in the section of the questionnaire asking for information about "affiliations of regional or local noteworthiness (such as positions with charitable fund-raising drives, activities with city, county or state; community, civic and welfare organizations)":

"Readings for benefit of Living Theatre in N.Y., Big Table Magazine, Chicago & Yugen Magazine in N.Y. & Measure Magazine in S.F. I do not accept gratuities (other than travel expense, if necessary) for poetry readings, which is curious if not noteworthy. I smoke a lot of marijuana and am a communist, more or less, tho an a-apolitical one, which is to say, mystical communism, if such exists."

On the question of "spouse," Ginsberg answered: "Peter Ganesh Orlofsky." "Date of Marriage: 1953, common law." In the space reserved for the details of the notable's military service, the pillar of the establishment wrote: "Copped out of World War II as 4-F, schizophrenic queer."

What Ginsberg was trying to accomplish in his autobiography is not without precedent in the *Who's Who* genre, although we have to go to England to find it. In the English *Who's Who*, which gives a man's recreations as a matter of course, George Bernard Shaw in an early volume listed "cycling and showing off." The Scottish poet Hugh McDiarmid gives his as "Anglophobia."

Few notables are as outspoken as Ginsberg. Still there is a way *Who's Who* can become more than just a dignified member of the vanity press. The editors, for example, could brighten their reference work by adding an editorial opinion section under each notable's straight news.

Of a "symph. orch. bassoonist" it could be said: "Began frittering away talents, 1965." Of a "psych." who turned to "motiv. rsch. with advtg. agy.": "He sold out, 1967." Of an "indust. tycn.": "Corp. really lost money, 1968. But his grndfthr. poured in fresh capital. Named corspndt. divorce suit, 1968. Also spent part 1968 in sanat. drying out."

Admittedly this will take some original research on the part of *Who's Who*. It will also take more pages. But there's no reason why *Who's Who* can't be two big volumes instead of one. As someone who has a stake in having this important reference work widely read by the American public, I hope the editors do *something* with Volume 36.

*Good
Intentions*

I'll never forget those long summers on Fire Island. Dozing in the warm sun on the white beach. Hearing flattering comments on the last book from friends of literature in bikinis. Catching up on the reading of other writers' books. Weighing invitations for martinis at five. The delicious dinners by hurricane lantern. Long romantic walks on the moonlit beaches.

Not that I ever did any of these wonderful things. I was too busy looking in the Ocean Beach sand dunes for my lost children, rushing to the drugstore for poison-ivy serum, waiting for an old homeowner to get a heart attack so I could get a game at one of the two tennis courts, and washing dishes. But I'll never forget those Fire Island summers anyway.

As I recall now, mostly they were a waste of valuable time.

A writer's summer vacation is the time to expand his mind as well as his ego. Around the Memorial Day weekend every year, I would begin packing a trunk of books on my required-reading list. As a free-lance without an area of specialization, I have to read an awful lot just to keep up with the field. But the road to Great South Bay is paved with good intentions. At the end of every summer the trunk of carefully chosen books would return to my home in New Jersey mildewed but unread. (I've often thought of pasting stickers on my books the way some people decorate their luggage.) But something happened this year that guarantees I won't be coming home from vacation with that old frustrated feeling.

By a stroke of bad fortune, I won't be leaving home in the first place. My last book was such a *succès d'estime* I can't afford to go back to Fire Island this summer—or even to Brighton Beach. Happily, I finally will have the time to get to all those books. I must be one of the luckiest writers in America today.

What will I be packing in my attaché case to read on the commuter bus rides from Leonia, New Jersey, to New York City? I plan to limit my reading this long hot summer to two kinds of books: prose and poetry. The only change in my reading plans for this summer is that everything on my list is specifically designed to meet my immediate needs.

This summer, for example, I won't be reading any books just for pleasure. Gibbon's *The Decline and Fall of the Roman Empire* was the first book off my list. Will Durant's *The Story of Civilization* and the outdated *War and Peace* also went from the trunk to the shelves.

"But you will be reading Thomas Mann's *The Magic Mountain?*" asked my wife as she put on the shelves a well-traveled copy of Plato's *Republic*.

"What's in it for me?"

"And how about the portable Dostoevsky you've been carrying to the shore the last five years?" she asked. "He's a very good writer."

"Yes, but did he ever meet a payroll!"

"And *Hamlet!*"

"I haven't been able to make up my mind about that one yet."

This summer I won't be wasting my time, either, reading books just because they have literary merit. That eliminates from my list *The Love Machine* by Jacqueline Susann, *Naked Came the Stranger* by Penelope Ashe, *My Life with Jacqueline Kennedy* by Mary Barelli Gallagher, *Miss Craig's 21-Day Shape-Up for Men and Women* by Marjorie Craig, *My Life and Prophecies* by Jeane Dixon and, especially, Norman Dacey's *How to Avoid Probate!* In order to have an estate to go into probate, you have to have at least sixty thousand dollars.

Then I put away the sociological studies, like Helen Gurley Brown's *Sex and the Single Girl* and *Sex and the Office,* which basically tell a reader how to meet men. That was one subject I didn't have to know anything about.

*Ulysses* by James Joyce went because I had recently read Judge Woolsey's decision calling it not obscene.

By the time I finished pruning I found that my trunk was almost empty.

What I needed was a reading list. Just reading books as they happen to interest a man is the mark of a disorganized mind. Fortunately, I've been collecting and filing away reading lists for years. It only took me several days to find the file.

In it I found the list of Haldeman-Julius Little Blue Books, a line of cheap (most sold for a nickel) paperbacks whose titles included *Best Jokes of 1937.* Since the Midwestern publisher went out of business, his books have all become camp classics. Obviously they would now be out of my financial range.

It did serve to remind me of another list of blue books—the Olympia Press catalog. Apparently I had filed that one so carefully, lest it fall into my kids' hands, that it was lost. Not that I would want to read any of those books today. When they had to be smuggled into the country from Paris, I really wanted to read every Olympia book; but the spice has gone out of the list since so many titles have been published by high-prestige houses like Grove Press.

Next I found "Reading List for English 49" and "Reading List for English 50," two courses Herman Wouk once taught as visiting professor of English at Yeshiva University. I've always been a great admirer of Herman Wouk's work. You should see the way he's fixed up his beach house in Seaview on Fire Island. But his lists were disappointing because they didn't include any books, like *Marjorie Morningstar*, which are essential for a writer's buying a home on Fire Island.

Clifton Fadiman included one of his books (*The American Treasury*) in his 100-book "The Lifetime Reading Plan"—thereby ranking himself with Homer, St. Augustine, Dante, Ibsen, Conrad, Thoreau, Dewey and Santayana, Marx and Freud. There's nothing immoral about that. Some of the country's most widely respected professors put their books on required reading lists. If I had been an obscure college teacher instead of a famous writer, you can bet my book would have been required reading for at least one course. And I'd be going on vacation this year instead of worrying about reading lists.

The most promising list in my files was published in 1945 under the title "A List of Books for Prospective Law Students Now in Service Prepared by a Committee of the Faculty of Harvard Law School." An introduction to the pamphlet explained that the list had been prepared in answer to "many requests from men in the armed forces who have not yet attended a law school, asking for advice on books which will help them decide about the desirability of entering the legal profession or which will be of value in the preparation for the study of law." Since one of the reasons I was in a financial hole was the contract I negotiated on my last book, I considered spending the summer reading the law. There were other good books on the Harvard list, too. Of the Bible, the faculty committee noted approvingly, "Read by Lincoln." Unfortunately, I next turned up a review of the list.

"To criticize any list of books put together for any purpose is something like shooting a bird," wrote Fred Rodell of the Yale University Law School in a 1945 issue of the *Yale Law Journal.* "It is not quite sporting, for any fool can do it. But the Harvard Law School's list is not a sitting bird. It is a dead bird. I write rather in the spirit of autopsy than in the spirit of sport." Professor Rodell's spirited analysis of the list found it guilty of including some books and omitting others.

Following the guidelines set down by Rodell, I saw that the same general criticism could be made of the remaining lists in my files, those compiled by Robert ("The Great Books of the Western World") Hutchins, Stringfellow Barr and Dr. Eliot of the original five-foot shelf of books. The only list that was beyond reproach seemed to be *Books in Print.* Edited by Sarah L. Prakken, the nineteenth annual edition (1966) simply lists all the 190,000 titles available today from *ABCDEFGHIJKLMNOPQRST- UVWXYZ* by Karla Kuskin to *Zymogram in Clinical Medicine* by S. H. Lawrence.

To make sure that she wouldn't have to

spend another summer at home, my wife culled for me the following required-reading list from *Books in Print: How to Make a Fortune Today, Starting from Scratch* by William Nickerson; *How to Win Success Before 40* by William G. Damroth; *How to Make $18,000 a Year Free-lance Writing* by L. D. Farrar; *How to Get Out of Debt and Enjoy Your Income* by J. Batista-Olivieri; and *How to Cash In on Your Hidden Memory Power* by William D. Hersey.

While I'm sure she has my own best interests at heart, I drafted another list from *Books in Print* which I plan to read on the side: *How to Live Well Without Working* by Philip White; *How to Make Money in One Day at the Track* by C. S. Romanelli; *How to Find a Real Hot Stock and a Blue-Nosed Open End No-Load Mutual Fund with No Salesman's Commission* by M. Bielawski; and *How and Where to Pan Gold* by W. Winters.

If the list is as good as it sounds, maybe I will be able to go on vacation this summer after all. Then I'll be packing a book titled *How to Be Rich* by J. Paul Getty.

---

Like George Bernard Shaw, Herbert Marshall McLuhan didn't write his first book until he was over forty. The obscure University of Toronto English professor's *The Mechanical Bride* was published in 1951, and largely ignored by everybody. This is a luxury few serious dilettantes can afford today. You can't just say you never trust anybody over forty. Now

*Get the Message?*

**83**

*everybody* has to have a position on McLuhan.

Current thinking on McLuhan's ideas is sharply divided. That is, some people think he is right; others think he is wrong. The majority, however, belongs to a third group, which public-opinion analysts sometimes call by the technical term "don't knows."

The truth is that in the seventeenth year of the McLuhan Age, which has revolutionized the thought processes of the post-Gutenberg man, a lot of people are still afraid to have any opinion about the great Canadian philosopher. This is understandable. Tom Wolfe explained that McLuhan is perhaps "the most important thinker since Newton, Darwin, Freud, Einstein and Pavlov." Many assume that the kind of appraisal necessary to arrive at an opinion about whether McLuhan is right or wrong would take years of close study.

I had that same misconception. For years I felt guilty about not coming to grips with the man's work. I used to dread the subject when it was raised at cocktail parties. When a girl asked me what I thought of a McLuhan point, like, "Schizophrenia may be a necessary consequence of literacy," I would answer: "I missed that one. *Damn* that Evelyn Woods course."

Thumbing through one of his books a few years ago, I came across an interesting McLuhan theorem. "As people become involved," he wrote, "the less they know."

He's got a very good point there, I said to myself. Later, when I applied the theory to McLuhan's work, I found it really held up in practice, too. I became fully relaxed about McLuhan. The less I knew about him, the greater was my understanding. Since conquering my irrational fears and anxieties, nothing gives me greater pleasure than turning other people on to him. So I've put down a few hints here which may help calm your fears about discovering the new world of Marshall McLuhan.

One way to get his message, of course, is to read his books. There are three major works: *The Mechanical Bride, The Gutenberg Galaxy* (1962) and *Understanding Media* (1964). If this is the way you want to go, there are several things you should know.

Don't be put off by McLuhan because he is difficult to understand. The reason so many critics have trouble with their basic McLuhan is that they give his books their undivided attention. I don't mind telling you—since I'm getting a fat fee for this article—that the secret of success with McLuhan is to give him your divided attention.

I always read him with the television set on, although I'm sure the radio or a hair dryer would work just as well. It is the mixing of media, McLuhan says, which makes children in this electronic age so smart.

Television hockey games, I've discovered, are an especially useful tool for increasing one's understanding of McLuhan. What we have here is the same environmental principle one finds in action when he drinks a glass of tea while reading Tolstoy's *War and Peace*. McLuhan, as I mentioned earlier, is a Canadian. Hockey is the national sport of Canada. I don't know whether McLuhan is a hockey fan or not (it is perhaps significant that hockey is one of the few subjects he doesn't make reference to in his works), but many of his chapters

**85**

read as if they had been written while *somebody* in McLuhan's house in suburban Toronto had the Maple Leafs game tuned in on the telly.

The primary offensive strategy in hockey is to shoot the puck into the opposition team's defensive zone. Then the attacking team rushes after the puck and sees what happens. On Madison Avenue this is called running an idea up the flagpole and seeing if anybody salutes. McLuhan calls his thought process "exploring."

"I am an investigator," he writes in a brief introduction to Gerald Emanuel Stearn's important anthology, *McLuhan: Hot & Cool*. "I make probes. I have no point of view, I do not stay in one position . . ." (Frank Mahavolich, the brilliant and eccentric center of the Toronto Maple Leafs, explained his style in essentially the same way, shortly before he had a nervous breakdown.) ". . . I don't explain—I explore."

At any rate, I gained so much confidence by giving McLuhan's books my divided attention that by March 1967 I was even able to consider accepting an assignment from *The New York Times Book Review* section to review his newest book. If it had been any other philosopher's book, I would have bowed out immediately, pleading ignorance. But I felt that I understood McLuhan as well as any of the other critics.

When the editor mentioned the name of the book, *The Medium Is the Massage*, it reminded me of what Sam Goldwyn once said: "If I want a massage, I go to Luxor Baths." But I agreed to look at the book anyway because I was curious about whether I had really gotten Mc-Luhan's message.

*The Medium Is the Massage* was a major publishing event in 1967. "For the first time," explained Jerry Agel, the "coordinator" of the book, "Marshall puts his message in terms everyone can understand. He is a genius." It was such a vital message, I also learned, Mc-Luhan and his associates broke with publishing tradition by publishing the paper edition even before the hard-cover. "We didn't have the time to wait a year," he explained, "to get Marshall's message into the hands of the ordinary people."

As was my way, I turned on the Stanley Cup hockey playoff game between the Montreal Canadiens and the New York Rangers, and began reading the paper version of *The Medium Is the Massage*. It took twenty-seven minutes. Next I read the hard-cover edition, containing the same text and pictures, only one and three quarters times larger and more than seven times as expensive. It also took twenty-seven minutes. When the media finished working me over completely, I found that I couldn't agree more with everything McLuhan had been saying all those years. We differed on one point: I naïvely thought the commercial was the message.

There was no longer any doubt in my mind that I was a McLuhanite. So I told *The New York Times Book Review* readers:

With all the zeal of a convert, I would like to urge everybody not to buy this book, in either the paper medium or cloth medium. McLuhan argues forcefully that the invention of television makes books obsolete. Anybody who purchases a McLuhan book is playing into the hands of McLuhan's enemies in the intellectual establishment; high sales figures can only tend to discredit him as a modern thinker. Besides, the invention of the Albert Schweitzer professorship, a $100,000 chair in the humanities McLuhan is to occupy at Fordham next semester, makes the need to buy his books obsolete. (If I'm wrong about any of the theories in this review so far, Mr. McLuhan, please understand that I'm only probing. By that I mean, I'm trying to think linearly. Before I fell under your influence, I reasoned circularly.)

"Does the publication of this book mean McLuhan has changed his mind about his seminal thought that books are obsolescent?" I asked the coordinator. "This book makes all other books on art and philosophy obsolete," Agel explained. "The message all the other reviewers are missing is that what we have here is a breakthrough book. It's the first book designed for the TV age."

For example, some of the scenes (or paragraphs) are printed upside down, like this one. In those terms, this is one of the most carelessly edited shows (or books) in mixed-media history. Still other scenes can be read only by holding the TV screen (or page) up to a mirror, as in this case. Once you have gone to the trouble, you're liable to remember the words of the great American critic Tallulah Bankhead, who said, "There is less here than meets the eye."

The proper way to study McLuhan's ideas is to watch them being presented on television.

Print, he says, is a "hot" medium; television is "cool." The television industry, however, is hot about McLuhan's ideas. What they like most is the one that says television is the most important medium in the electric age. This is like telling an ugly woman she is beautiful.

As a result, a major network gave McLuhan an hour to explain his message. Unfortunately, the NBC show went on the air in March 1967. This is no problem for the now people with home videotape-recorder rigs and the foresight to have taped it. Screen the tape now. You won't be able to put the tape down until you've finished viewing it.

Keep in mind that the invention of Marshall McLuhan has made obsolete the way we judge a man's ideas on television. It is no longer possible to use the old-fashioned criteria to form your opinions; it is not *what* he says that is important, but *how* he says it. If the medium *is* the message, one must use such new criteria as: (1) If a philosopher's eyes are closely set, he looks sneaky, and (2) Be suspicious of the man who doesn't look you in the eye while he talks to you.

McLuhan opened his discussion of McLuhanism by looking at my refrigerator in the kitchen. He looked at my dog sleeping in the corner of the living room. He even noticed that my wife still hadn't made the beds upstairs at 4 P.M. In the sixty minutes of this otherwise laudable television show, he never once looked me in the eye. I bet he even had sweaty palms.

This may explain why I finally found a few of McLuhan's concepts questionable. For instance, he argues that television is a more superior educational tool than a book. If he is right, it means every parent who yells to a child, "Shut off that damn television set and do your homework," is wrong. The modern parent who wants his kids to get into a good college will have to warn, "Candy and books are bad for you." Otherwise, tomorrow's high-school graduates will have trouble answering an important question on college entrance applications: "List several television shows you have watched lately."

It is also hard to accept his idea that computers are modern man's enemy, in the sense that the "electrically computerized dossier bank" is a gossip column. It may be true for the person who has something to hide. But the fact that computers know all about us is not a total evil, at least for many lonely Americans. It proves that someone out there *cares*.

But there I go falling into the old trap of discussing the message instead of the medium again.

The third, and most effective, medium for getting McLuhan's message is the telephone.

If the wheel is an extension of the foot, as the professor correctly reports, and the book is an extension of the eye, then the telephone must be an extension of the ear. According to McLuhan, the spoken word is the most emotional form of communication. But to have a really meaningful communication experience, it is necessary to establish a connection.

When I raised this problem in my *Times* review, I solved it by including Marshall McLuhan's private telephone number at the University of Toronto along with a recommendation that readers ask him directly for the message.

Random House was charging ten dollars for McLuhan's message in its laughably fifteenth-century media. Bantam Books was charging $1.45 for its pitifully dated media. But the swinging people at AT&T were charging only eighty cents for a long-distance message (the station-to-station rate from New York). I advised serious students to call him after 6 P.M.

If anybody wanted to show the professor they really understood the workings of media, they might call "collect."

This would have been an absurd proposal in 1964, when McLuhan published his definitive work, *Understanding Media*. The message was still well hidden. In the current rendition, I had it on good authority that he had boiled down the message to 17 words. "The message, and why it had to get out now, is on page 25," advised coordinator Agel. "But pages 26 and 148 are very important, too."

In three minutes on the phone, McLuhan could easily give a person the whole message, and still have time to throw in a couple of one-liners, like: "Casting my perils before swains."

It seemed like such a sound, modern way to get the message into the ears of the people that, in view of the urgency, I was surprised that McLuhan hadn't thought of it himself. When he had to leave his office, he could have left the message with his secretary. If he got bored with teaching, he could have used another wonder of the electronic-circuitry age, the recorded message. And if there was no answer in Toronto, the people could always call a medium and ask her for a message.

Later I learned that 327 *New York Times* readers followed my advice and called the professor concerning his message. While this may sound impressive, more than a million people went out and bought the book. I never realized how widespread was the movement to destroy McLuhan.

I found out about these facts in a curious way. Several months after the review appeared, I received a mysterious phone call at my office in New Jersey. "Will you accept a call from a Mr. Marshall McLuhan?" the operator asked. She added that he was calling from San Francisco, and that it was collect.

"It depends on what he has to say," I answered noncommittally. "I'm familiar with his work."

The operator said she couldn't find out what his message was in advance. I explained that I was a starving writer, but a phone call would hardly make a dent in Professor McLuhan's stipend at Fordham. "Money is a metaphor," I said, repeating one of the important McLuhan thoughts memorized earlier in my studies.

Mr. McLuhan answered, "The medium is the message."

While I argued with the operator about how I didn't think the phone call sounded like it would be worth much, and that I definitely hadn't accepted it, Mr. McLuhan went right on talking. He announced what he claimed was good news: "You've been awarded the Electric Chair in Canadian Literature at Fordham."

This was confirmed by another voice. It sounded like Father John Culkin, S.J., director of the School of Communications at Fordham, but I wouldn't swear to it. There was so much confusion with the three of us talking. When two other voices entered the conversation, it became obvious that a collect conference call was taking place. The phone company was going to get stuck with a big bill.

Mr. McLuhan monopolized the conversation, quoting liberally from the truths in his books. Occasionally I tried to hold up my end of the conversation, saying things like, "The invention of eyeglasses makes lasagna obsolete."

"What?" he asked.

A little less sure of myself, I answered, "The invention of the Pullman car makes the draft lottery obsolete."

My intellectual hero said a lot of things, most of which were beneath the dignity of his high office. I still don't know what he was so mad about.

Jack Gould puzzled in his *New York Times* review: "Has overexposure in the television age already cut short the McLuhan influence?" I think not; it's just beginning.

The other night I explained to my wife, "The invention of the home videotape-recorder rig makes Jack Gould obsolete."

"What?" replied my wife.

"I've got it. The invention of the camera makes conspicuous consumption obsolete."

"It's getting late," she said.

"The idea is that rich people need to impress poor people that they're superior. The rich distinguish themselves by their ability to be in contact with each other. For example, poor people can't see the rich people's art collections. But the invention of the camera, which makes pictures of the art for *Life* magazine, exposes everybody to everything. . . ."

"Turn off the lights. It's 3 A.M."

"What about this one? The invention of your father makes my getting a regular job obsolete."

"You finally have something," she conceded.

## The Honorable Art of Dits and Dabs

The only truly native American contribution to *belles-lettres* is telegram writing. When the telegram was first introduced as an art form in America on May 24, 1844, by an obscure writer named Samuel F. B. Morse, it immediately gave rise to some of the best prose in the American idiom. Letter writing became mere journalism compared to telegram writing. The immortal words of Samuel Morse, such as . . . . -- -- . . . , were widely repeated all over the world. Some of the best American writers of yesterday wrote telegrams. Yet, today, American writers who have something urgent to say neglect telegram writing. To understand the causes of this alienation we must first take a closer look at the art form.

Telegram writing requires more discipline than writing haiku. As an art form, it demands that the writer use only fifteen words, Western Union's basic telegram rate. Haiku writers must say everything in seventeen syllables. Thus, telegram writing is even richer in hidden meanings, subtleties and symbolism. As I first observed in the *Hudson Street Review*, one telegram is worth a thousand words.

This is not to imply that the telegram form does not lend itself to poetic ambiguity. Elimination of the mere article "the" in a telegram can instantaneously create the kind of confusion so desirable in art. As Professor Neil Postman, director of New York University's Linguistics Demonstration Center, correctly points out, "SHIP SAILS TOMORROW" could mean "SHIP THE SAILS TOMORROW" or "THE SHIP SAILS TOMORROW." The telegram as proletarian poetry has also benefited from confusion, as in "STRIKE WHILE THE IRON IS HOT." Is this a

94

proverb, or instructions from a union's international executive committee to an ironworkers' local, regarding the best time to cripple an industry? It is a well-known fact that such ambiguity is the essence of poetry. But where poetry writers are limited to only seven types of ambiguity, according to the critic Empson, telegram writers have *eleven* types of ambiguity to experiment with.

Critics have differed in placing the blame for the decline of telegram writing as poetry. My inclination is to blame the Western Union Company for not understanding the message in Samuel Morse's early work. Morse's deep desire for simplicity of language was a reaction against the flowery New England Transcendentalists, who dominated the literary Establishment. Unlike the chatterboxes Thoreau, Emerson, and especially Whitman, Morse loved the brief, the clear, the bold, a style personified in his code. The Morse code was popular with the avant-garde not only because it pruned the deadwood out of the language, but because it couldn't be understood by the masses.

Despite Western Union's blunder—it abandoned Morse's style after discovering delivery boys couldn't sing in Morse code—telegram writing as an art form survived to some extent. That is because the telegram traditionally is associated in the public's mind with good news. When the average American receives a telegram his first reaction is that he is about to inherit a hundred thousand dollars.

The key to the telegram's durability undoubtedly lies in its ability to engage the emotions more directly than the sonnet. I'll never

**95**

forget the emotional involvement I experienced the first time I received a telegram from the President of the United States. It read, "GREETINGS."

With such a rich cultural heritage, why then do so many of today's promising young writers fear to write for the telegram? Some novelists shy away from this art form because they have nothing important to say. They have no message. That flaw is more easily disguised in the novel than in the telegram. On the other hand, some new poets and playwrights fear telegram writing because it exposes them as not being obscure enough.

As my contribution to the cultural explosion in this country, I have been trying to revive telegram writing. The Japanese government encourages haiku writing as part of its national cultural heritage. If American telegram writing is to flourish once again—as it did before air mail and long-distance telephoning became so popular—it, too, will need government support. I have been pioneering government subsidies for young telegram writers by sending telegrams to public officials collect. These telegrams are of the school of protest and are particularly well received at the White House. President Johnson didn't act until he found out what the public was thinking. A telegram speeds up the collective process of reaching a consensus. President Nixon is just as open. His office once accepted a wire from me which read: "IF YOU DON'T ACCEPT COLLECT TELEGRAMS, DON'T ACCEPT THIS ONE."

I have also sponsored telegram readings in Greenwich Village coffeehouses. More than poetry, telegrams are meant to be read aloud.

Witness how telegrams are presented at weddings, confirmations and bar mitzvahs and over the telephone. And knowing that the future of any art form depends on appreciation by the young, I have also been urging elementary school teachers to assign essays on the subject "My First Telegram."

Progress is already discernible in my campaign to get creative people to write more for the telegram. It was my missionary work which made a Hollywood producer first tell a screenwriter: "Pictures are for entertainment; if I want a message I use Western Union."

Lest any of my enemies in literary criticism accuse me of ulterior motives in reviving telegram writing, I would like to assure the reader that my interest in this worth-while endeavor is as high-minded as any other stockholder in the Western Union Telegraph Company. It was my suggestion at the last stockholders' meeting that the company could aid telegram writing as an art form by insisting that all sentences include a subject, verb and object, at the same time banning messages which said things between the lines.

---

Studies I am doing in Comparative Campaign Lit 1 are in an early stage, and it is perhaps premature to publish, but the inaugural tomorrow (January 20, 1969) brought to mind Richard Nixon's moving promise to his wife to quit politics for good in 1956. A little less than half the American voters may be curious about why the President did not fulfill that promise. The old Nixon (*Richard Nixon: A Political and Per-*

*Comparative Lit 1*

*sonal Portrait*), written by Earl Mazo and published in 1959, goes into it at some length:

> When I asked Nixon long afterwards why he changed his mind about leaving politics, he said it was "circumstances" more than any particular event. "Pat felt very, very strongly about it," he explained. "Ever since the fund thing she hasn't been keen on this business." Then he added:
>
> "Once you get into this stream of history you can't get out. You can drown. Or you can be pulled ashore by the tide. But it is awfully hard to get out when you are in the middle of the stream—if it is intended that you stay there."

For some reason these paragraphs, the subject of which was later to play such a major role in Hubert Humphrey's setback last November, were omitted from the new *Nixon* (*Nixon: A Political Portrait*), written by Earl Mazo and Stephen Hess and published in July of 1968.

I can understand Mazo and Hess's motivation in de-emphasizing Nixon's promise to Pat. Every man makes promises to his wife which he forgets about fifteen minutes later, even when, as in Nixon's case, he takes the trouble to write the decision down on a piece of paper and puts it inside his wallet. (The "circumstances" that helped change the then Vice President's mind, as revealed in the old *Nixon:* President Eisenhower asked him to run again in 1956.) But why should the authors of the new *Nixon* have chosen to delete a paragraph that quotes Nixon saying in 1954 to Murray M. Chotiner, the Beverly Hills lawyer, publicist and political adviser: " 'Here is my last campaign speech. You may like to keep it as a souvenir.' Then, as if to show he was serious, Nixon discussed the relative merits of opening his own law office or joining an established firm."

While I'm on the subject: my statistics (based on incomplete returns) show that forty-eight lines about Chotiner, Nixon's first political guru (under this miracle man, Nixon was undefeated in politics, which is more than can be said for his later advisers), disappeared from the new *Nixon*. Is this any way to treat a good friend of the new President?

"Late in May the name of Murray Chotiner, Nixon's campaign manager, came up in a Senate investigating committee's investigation of a garment manufacturer accused of stealing government property," the old *Nixon* reported exclusively. "Chotiner was his lawyer. Nixon was in no way implicated. But every news story tied Chotiner to him. This delighted those still anxious to bypass Nixon's nomination [in 1956] and caused the Vice President to sever his political relationship with his ingenious campaign technician." Chotiner's political ghost still hovers over Nixon. Chotiner played an important role in explaining what a politician could do with television. If in the next few months the new President appears on home screens as the genial host of a televised meeting of the (secret) National Security Council, we can thank Murray Chotiner. As a result of Nixon's search for the best-qualified men for jobs in the new Administration—a talent hunt which began with the selection of Spiro Agnew as his running mate—Chotiner may soon appear in Washington—maybe even as a Justice of the Supreme Court.

Frankly, I am embarrassed to be commenting on these differences between the old and the new *Nixon*s. It sounds too much like scholarly nitpicking. But these questions may be hotly argued by graduate students some fifty years from now, and the collection of quotes and facts that I've gathered by reading the books side by side, paragraph by paragraph, may still be useful.

Both of these books are in the genre technically known as "the unauthorized campaign biography," an art form which, like politics itself, combines nonfiction and fiction. It dates back to Mason Locke Weems's best seller of 1799, *The Life of Washington the Great, Enriched with a number of Very Curious Anecdotes, Perfectly in Character, and Equally Honorable to Himself and Exemplary to his Young Countrymen*. Eventually this book went through eighty editions into this century. The new *Nixon* is now in its fourth printing, and may be the first serious challenger the *Washington* has ever had. Much depends on the Nixon administration, of course, as to whether people want to remember or forget it. But together the two *Nixon*s have already had a life span far greater than the usual campaign biography.

The reappearance of *Nixon*, like Lazarus, was such an unusual thing in publishing that the authors introduced it with a note: "We think that in at least one respect this book is a unique undertaking," Mazo and Hess wrote in the new *Nixon*. "It is a book based on a book. Or, in architectural terms, it might be considered a new building raised on an existing foundation." In literary terms, what this means is that Mazo and Hess have slightly altered the second through fourteenth stories, or chapters. (The last six chapters, which cover the President's career since 1959, are new.) The early chapters contain some new facts which apparently weren't available in 1959, such as the information that Richard Nixon could whip mashed potatoes better than the other Nixon boys (no lumps). But by and large the creative energy in chapters two to fourteen has gone into deleting material.

One of the few people with whom I thought I could have an intelligent discussion about the significance of what was left out of the new *Nixon* was Stephen Hess. It was widely assumed that the condensations were done by Earl Mazo, since Mazo, a former *New York Herald Tribune* reporter, is now an editor with the *Reader's Digest*. But I learned through the publishing grapevine that Hess was in charge of the revisions.

Hess worked for President Eisenhower as a special assistant in 1959 and 1960. "In effect, I was the No. 2 speech writer at the White House," he explained. Mark Harris mentions in his book *Mark the Glove Boy, or the Last Days of Richard Nixon*, about the Nixon California gubernatorial race in 1962, that Hess served as staff intellectual. ("Like others of Mr. Nixon's staff, Hess had joined in skepticism and grown to passion.") He is also a fellow at the Institute of Political Science, John F. Kennedy School of Government, at Harvard. His role in Cambridge, it has been said, is that of "Republican-in-residence."

"I've been reading the old *Nixon*," I explained when I reached Hess at his home in Washington two weeks before Inauguration Day. He was sitting by the phone.

"Why would anybody want to do that?" he asked suspiciously.

To demonstrate that I had done my homework, I asked: "Do you remember the footnote in the new *Nixon*, the one on page 121, about what happened after the Vice President made that great speech on TV to explain the fund thing and he asked the people to write or wire the Republican National Committee to express their feelings about him?" Hess said he didn't remember it exactly. I read the footnote verbatim from the new *Nixon* to refresh his memory:

All the messages were never totaled. Party headquarters in Washington, alone, got 300,000 letters, cards, telegrams and petitions, signed altogether by a million people. They have been given to Whittier College, where Dr. Robert W. O'Brien has studied them for clues to sociological motivations. Underclassmen have dubbed the huge collection "The Dead Sea Scrolls."

He said he remembered it now. "But in the old *Nixon*," I went on, "the footnote read:

All the messages were never totaled. Party headquarters in Washington, alone, got 300,000 letters, cards, telegrams and petitions, signed altogether by a million people. They have been given to Whittier College, where Dr. Robert W. O'Brien, head of the sociology department, and Mrs. Elizabeth Jensen Jones, an associate, are studying them for clues to sociological motivations. Underclassmen have dubbed the huge collection "The Dead Sea Scrolls."

"What happened to Mrs. Jones? Did she lose interest in the project between 1952 and 1968?"

"What would you want to know anything like that for?" Hess asked in a tone he probably once used with Drew Pearson. I explained that I was trying to do a study on the old and new *Nixon*s before all the action started on Capitol Hill on Inaugural Day and everything got confused. "Was there anything else different about the new *Nixon*?"

"Mazo uses a lot of contractions," Hess explained. "Like *won't* and *don't*, which I changed."

"I mean was there any special significance to your eliminating the paragraph about how Nixon in 1952 went to the Wisconsin convention and gave Senator Joseph McCarthy an endorsement?"

Hess said that he had to cut somewhere. The new *Nixon* couldn't be a weighty historical tome. He had to fit in the new chapters he previously had written about Nixon for an earlier book of his, entitled *The Republican Establishment*. He deleted whatever seemed irrelevant. "Chotiner? He happened to be in one of the areas we tightened."

"What Chotiner said after Ike's advisers were ready to dump Nixon before the Checkers speech, so they could save the TV expense, was one of the most dramatic moments in the old *Nixon*. I reminded him: 'If Dick is off the ticket, all the printing you'll have to do over again will cost you a lot more money than a television program.' It gave Dick the chance to make good."

"We cut pages out of the South American adventure," he reminded me. "Dick looked very heroic in Colombia, Bolivia and Peru against those Communist students in 1958. Mrs. Nixon was very heroic, too."

While we were discussing personalities instead of issues, there was Harold Stassen, who even more than Chotiner suffered from Hess's cutbacks. Some 619 lines about his role as a major force in the Republican Party and as Nixon's early political mentor had been cut (even the parenthetical note that it was Stassen who delivered the votes at the 1952 convention to put Ike over the top had vanished). Who would still believe that in the old *Nixon* Harold Stassen was one of the foreign-policy advisers Nixon had invited to the White House? Why had Stassen become such an unperson in the new *Nixon?* Stassen made mistakes as a politician, the worst being his decision to debate Dewey in Oregon. But what Republican hadn't?

A thing that fascinated me was Nixon's remark that "President Eisenhower would have made a very fine lawyer. He doesn't have what usually gets a poor lawyer into trouble—the one-track mind. . . ." Did you ask Nixon about his opinion on that judgment before you dropped it? "As a general rule," Hess explained, "it was easier and quicker to cut material than try and find the candidate in New Hampshire or wherever he was campaigning. This book was put together in a hurry."

I hope it wasn't negligence that caused Hess to keep many of the finest parts of the old *Nixon* in the new *Nixon*. We relive the days when Nixon was the so-called bayonet of the Republican Party, demonstrating his expertise in the fields of innuendo and what the Democratic newspapers used to call "smear tactics." But not all of the many examples in the old *Nixon* have survived, including my favorite Mazoism:

**104**

Nixon was always a fast man on the uptake. He

reached a peak of nimbleness, however, in his re-tort to Stevenson's assertion that Nixon repre-sented "McCarthyism in a white collar." That, declared Nixon, was an attack on the working people. "What Mr. Stevenson calls me is unimpor-tant," he stated, "but I resent his typically snide and snobbish innuendo toward the millions of Americans who work for a living in our shops and factories."

The only reason I could think of for cutting out such things was that times have changed. Those were the bad old days, the post-Korean War period, when the government was riddled with sex perverts, alcoholics, traitors and other undesirable subversive elements. Never-theless, should the nation someday want to look into who was responsible for losing the war in Vietnam (*which* intellectuals and egg-heads, as they used to say), Nixon's past would come in handy.

Hess seemed more at ease discussing pub-lishing history than the history of the changes in the two *Nixon*s. "There was no Nixon book until I got the idea about how it could be done fast. Nobody wanted a Nixon book. They had five Romney biographies in the works. The New York intellectual establishment couldn't fathom Nixon. I kept telling them Nixon was going to win." The only disappointing thing to Hess is that the book hasn't sold as well as he had hoped.

Did Nixon like the new *Nixon?*

"They didn't buy the plates," he said. "There was no Nixon subsidy on this book."

I said I meant artistically. Apparently he did. At least he didn't complain, according to Hess. "I heard through the grapevine he liked it very much. He sent me a letter saying something like 'I haven't read it yet. But everybody around the office said it is even better than the original book, which was very good.' He has a new sophistication in dealing with the press. He doesn't expect unqualified approval any more. He's much more plausible. If on balance he comes out well, he now feels he is ahead of the game."

I apologized for tying up Hess's phone line so long. "Yes, I was talking to some people about going to work for the new administration. I am an inner-and-outer. I leave to write a book every so often to charge my batteries." During the last presidential campaign, about which he has just finished writing an epilogue for the next edition of the new *Nixon*, Hess worked for the Nixon team. His job, I have heard, was serving as one of the three men assigned to advise Spiro Agnew on the problems of misquotation. I promise to read his *Agnew* as carefully as his *Nixon*.

---

## On Making an Ashe Out of Yourself

For years various disciplines have been studying the effects of television on viewers. Eye doctors are trying to find out how TV effects the eyes. Radiologists are looking for the impact of loose X rays. Few people, however, are examining the effects of the medium in the area of vocational guidance.

Lawyers, doctors, and detectives have had their day. My guess is that the "in" vocation among the young this year is novelists. The current trend in thinking about the field is that you don't need talent to succeed.

This is in marked contrast to the old days

(1965). Then it was widely assumed that you had to be particularly brilliant and especially ruthless to earn a million dollars or so. We live in the era of the common man and woman in the literary arts. If she could do it, the average television viewer looking at the guests on the talk shows says to himself, by God I can do it, if I had the time and motivation. Nobody really worries about the lack of talent any more.

Actually we have this kind of trend on television every time Jacqueline Susann writes a novel. Unlike most talk-show guests, she is always being asked to discuss her credentials as a writer, not her work. Miss Susann is a good sport about it, never appearing to mind going over the same old ground with her harshest critics, as long as they mention the name of her latest book.

Jackie Susann Month on national television —now in its eighth week—will have even greater impact this year (1969) because of another major television event, the presentation of *Youngblood Hawke* on *CBS Friday Night Movies.*

*Youngblood Hawke,* if you recall the 1962 reviews, is Herman Wouk's powerful and lengthy (783 pages) statement about the mechanics of writing novels. It is the story of a Kentucky truck driver whose gifts as a writer enable him to rocket to success overnight. As I watched the television show, I was reminded of the time in my life when I was unduly influenced by the movie's content.

That I identified with James Franciscus, who played the title role in the Warner Brothers film, was not surprising. We were both good-looking, articulate, dynamic men. But it still makes me nervous recalling how I almost walked out of *Youngblood Hawke* before it had a chance to work its magic.

The movie dragged a little in its first ten minutes. The hero only finished his first thousand-page novel, quit his job in Kentucky as a truck driver, flew to New York by jet by order of a top publisher, signed a contract in a plush skyscraper, agreed to accept the help of a beautiful editor (Suzanne Pleshette) on his second book, and found a picturesque apartment in Brooklyn Heights with a view of the New York skyline at sixty dollars a month.

That sequence of events in the life of the average American writer was so commonplace as to be painfully boring. At the eleven-minute mark, Wouk's movie suddenly came to life.

Still in his old Kentucky clothes, Mr. Hawke is dragged by his beautiful editor to an eggnog party at the home of his publisher. A gorgeous blonde millionairess (Genevieve Page), with three kids at home (I don't remember their names) somewhere in Connecticut, confessed that from the moment she saw the writer walk through the door she had an uncontrollable desire to cook sausages and eggs for him at her lower Fifth Avenue *pied-à-terre*.

As soon as he enters the mansion, the truth strikes Mr. Hawke. She only wanted him in the house because of his ability as a novelist. Drugged by her way around the gas range and kitchen sink, he accidentally seduces the millionairess. He quickly apologizes and pledges he will never do anything like that again.

Well, I knew enough about the art of writing a novel to know this scene was a metaphor. In real life beautiful rich women don't cook meals for writers: they send out to Max's Kansas City or the Dover Delicatessen.

Within ten minutes Mr. Hawke moved into a rent-free garret in the artists-and-writers quarter of New York, Sutton Place. Although the picture was only half over, I was seized with the wild desire to rush out of the theater. I had to find a typewriter so I could immediately begin my first novel.

It was one o'clock in the morning and my wife tried to discourage me from writing the whole thousand-page novel at a single sitting. She was worried about my health. But as Youngblood Hawke himself put it, "the words they just came a-pourin' out."

Nothing much happened after that, except women started chasing me at cocktail parties. I would be standing there minding my own business, but then I'd accidentally say something about my novel—a transition problem, say, on page 43—and they would get a wild look in their eyes. The unmarried women were the really impossible ones. Every time I mentioned my troubles writing a simple sentence, some girl would ask me for my phone number.

The problem with my novel was that what was selling in 1965 was unadulterated rot. As a friend of mine explained, I could only write adulterated rot. Watching *Youngblood Hawke* on CBS started an old wound twitching. I thought of all those young fellows in the audience rushing off to slave over a novel, which at this time in the history of the novel could be disastrous.

The emergence of Penelope Ashe, the authoress of record of *Naked Came the Stranger*, is more painful evidence of how hard work doesn't pay off. On her most recent appearance on the David Frost show, the Dick Cavett of England introduced television's writing fool as "the most extraordinary authoress in America." The spotlight went on the curtain. "Let's have a hand for a many-sided authoress," Frost said, as the curtain parted and the twenty-five co-authors from *Newsday* walked out on stage and took their bows. Miss Ashe (played by a Mrs. Billie Young) followed in their wake, eating up the applause.

"Where did all of this amazing editorial project start?" Frost asked Harvey Aronson, the Long Island newspaperman who with the Nieman Fellow Mike McGrady is the widely acknowledged ringleader of this shameless hoax perpetrated on the American people.

"Given the time—a week," Aronson answered, "—we felt we could write a truly bad book."

It's not as easy as those twenty-five guys are making it sound, I found myself crying out to the unthinking TV audience swallowing all of this nonsense as I had taken Herman Wouk's bitter draft. Some people can write a bad book in a week. Some people can't.

Penelope Ashe said she didn't think *Naked Came the Stranger* was such a bad book. "It's a great parody of American marriage," she said, seriously.

"Don't listen to her," Aronson broke in sharply. "She doesn't know what she's talking about. This is a terrible book. It can't miss."

"They knock it," Miss Ashe said of the critics, who had each written a chapter. "But I think it's a beautiful book."

Here at last was the first real conflict in the novel. In front of millions of potential aspiring novelists, the team of twenty-five novelists and a front woman were fighting like a pack of thieves over the literary merits of *Naked Came the Stranger!*

While this must have struck many future novelists as pure fiction—a conflict like this could keep the novel before the public eye for as much as an extra week—I learned from an informed source that it is a sincere difference of opinion. A sportswriter at *Newsday*, a 1/25 partner in the project whose chapter was too good to be included, said that Penelope Ashe really believes in the novel. In fact, she is at work on her second novel, which may be called *Naked Came the Stranger Again* or *Naked Came Another Stranger*. The poor woman has fallen under the influence of the Jackie Susann syndrome watching too much television.

I don't want to get involved in literary disputes. But in my opinion the real hoax aspect in the *Naked Came the Stranger* chapter of literary history is that one of those reporters wrote a first novel, which no publisher would touch because it was too promising, thus doomed to fail. So he fell back on his imagination and invented the twenty-five-men-and-a-girl story, a beautiful gimmick.

David Frost did nothing to cool off the boom in new novelists by inviting a row in the balcony of the Little Theatre on West Forty-fourth Street, where his show is taped, to write their own novel. He supplied these novices with a paragraph-long premise, and asked each member of the row to add a line to keep the plot moving.

This was Frost's premise:

"A glorious pulse was pounding in her throat as Ned moved toward the closet where Ralph was hiding. She stifled a scream as Ned threw open the closet door and said:"

The first person in the row wrote:

"Ralph, what are you doing in one of Gloria's dresses?"

(2) Without answering, Ralph grabbed Gloria by the bedpost and kissed her repeatedly along the neck.

(3) "Stop, Ralph," said Gloria. "Not in front of Ned."

(4) Ralph grabbed Ned by the bedpost and kissed him repeatedly along the neck.

(5) Ralph grabbed the bed by the bedpost and kissed it repeatedly along the headboard.

(6) "Stop, Ralph," said Ned. "Not in front of the chair."

(7) Suddenly, a shot rang out and a naked form came crashing through the window.

(8) "It's Supernude," said Gloria.

My message to those balcony novelists is this:

I have a publisher for your novel. If you'll please contact me, I can get you a healthy advance, plus solid royalties, with a possible three-picture deal thrown in.

Television has taught me that my real vocation is as a literary agent.

---

## The Perils of Publishing

While reading Robert Gutwillig's essay "Reflections of a Publisher" (*New Leader*, December 5, 1966), I found myself vaguely wondering what a publisher really knows about publishing. But I didn't understand my uneasiness until I read author Leonard Baker's letter to the editor (*NL*, Jan. 2, 1967). "Magazines always turn to publishers to answer the question of what is wrong with publishing," he wrote. "That's like asking a lawyer what's wrong with your liver."

It occurred to me that the only way to keep a discussion about publishing on a high level is to turn the job over to an objective authority, somebody with perspective, an author who has just received his first royalty statement. I meet these rigid requirements.

Rather than discuss all the twenty-eight thousand books published last year, however, which would lead only to confusion on my part, I will limit my reflections to what I consider the most important book published in 1966. By that I mean my first book.

Before I wrote my book, I tried to figure out the secret for making it a number one best seller. I took a look at *The New York Times Book Review* list of best sellers one Sunday, which looked about the same then as now.

One way to get on the list was to write something literary, like Jacqueline Susann's *Valley of the Dolls*, Harold Robbins' *The Adventurers* or James Michener's *The Source*, an epic of warm lovable Jewish families from 38 B.C. to the present. But I realized that I wasn't really a literary kind of writer.

Other best sellers on the list seemed to have some kind of institutional support. Cornelius Ryan's *The Last Battle*, for example, had all the research facilities of *Reader's Digest* behind it. *Reader's Digest* has thousands of tape recorders, some of which automatically con-

**113**

dense whatever they hear. *Unsafe at Any Speed* by Ralph Nader had the full cooperation of the automobile industry and General Motors.

Finally, I coldly calculated the kind of story that would appeal to major motion-picture producers, TV-special makers, the drama and musical-comedy stage. I decided to write the story of my life. I was smart enough, though, to know that without any special literary gifts or big organizations behind me the odds were against my book ever becoming the number one best seller. To make sure that my dreams as a writer would come true, I called it *The Number One Best Seller*.

Drury's book, Wallace's book or Susann's book might be called "the number one best seller" this week, but who knew what they would be called next week? No matter how literary tastes changed over the years, my book would always be *The Number One Best Seller* (Library of Congress Catalog Number: 66-12827). Even when it reached the remainder stores.

But my problems were just beginning. The publisher was pressing me for the manuscript. Dial Press had invested only five thousand dollars in the book, and within days they seemed to be questioning their judgment. My editor, Henry Robbins, who discovered me in the pages of the *Saturday Evening Post*, either jumped or fell up to a job as editor-in-chief at Farrar, Straus & Giroux before I wrote a single word. I had heard a lot about how important editors were in the publishing business, and I thought it was my usual good luck to have three of them during the critical stage of producing my book, the writing.

The raw materials we had to work with were a series of magazine articles dealing with my adventures in Wall Street, the CIA, public service, foreign affairs and politics. The only trouble with the stories, explained my new editor, Christopher Lehmann-Haupt, was that once they were bound together they would constitute a collection. Everybody in publishing knew that collections don't sell. As an outsider, all I knew about was *Please Don't Eat the Daisies.*

My editor told me to make a single narrative out of the stories. "What readers want to know," he advised, "is *why* you wanted to corner the market in Imperial Chinese Government Hukuang Railways Sinking Fund Gold Loan 5½ percent of 1911 bonds. *Why* you wanted to be President."

"I already told them in the article that I'd rather be President than write," I protested. He grimly said, "Collections don't sell."

I don't know the philosophies of other freelance writers, but around my house my wife is always saying, "Publish—or perish." I would perish if I didn't follow Lehmann-Haupt's advice; the word would spread to other editors that I was one of those temperamental writers. And I would perish trying to live on Dial's advance. My editor seemed to know what he was talking about, so I followed his advice. Within the year it took to write my memoirs, I managed to become the economic equal of my cleaning woman, before I fired her on the flimsy excuse that I could no longer afford her services.

Like all good editors, Lehmann-Haupt

**115**

moved to a new job—at *The New York Times Book Review*—just as I finished the manuscript. He assured me that the new editor, E. L. Doctorow, understood my work and all would be well. But I was suspicious of Doctorow after the first month. Everytime I had an editorial conference with him a doubt lingered in my mind: What kind of guy could he be if nobody was hiring him away from Dial? I felt a lot better about his ability after learning that Dial had hired *him* away from New American Library for more money.

"Your manuscript doesn't work," he said one day. Seeing how disappointed I was, he quickly added, "But we may be able to save it. I'll call you in a few days to let you know what's wrong with it."

If my new editor had any flaws, it was the time he took to make decisions. Several weeks later, he called and said, "The part where you describe your early life is funny, but take it out." I didn't say anything. "The part where you go into your schooling is also funny, but it has to go."

He eventually recommended that I cut out all the connecting fabric I had been instructed to weave into my memoirs. "What you have to do," he said firmly, "is make a collection out of it."

Differences of editorial opinion are everyday occurrences in the publishing world, and a writer has no right to complain. "If you can't stand the heat in the kitchen," author Harry Truman once said, "get the hell out." I fought for my version anyway.

But Doctorow really seemed to know what he was talking about. It only took me two days to eliminate a year's hard work. And it was worth the pain and anguish just to hear my editor finally say, several weeks after I delivered the revised manuscript: "You're another Thurber."

"Are you sure?" I asked nervously. "I may be another Benchley, but I don't think a Thurber."

Doctorow, who is known in the trade as "Easy Ed" for his ability to stay calm in the storms of authorial temper, looked me straight in the eye. "That's just what I said. You're the new Benchley." He crossed out "Thurber" and wrote "Benchley" into the draft of the jacket copy for my book. I'm mentioning this now not merely to illustrate how publishers curry favor with authors. The few who have actually read my book may be curious about how I became known as "the Benchley of the 1960s."

Naturally, I wanted my editor to like me, too. He had implied that he knew even more about selling a book than about editing. His first book, *Welcome to Hard Times*, had just been sold to the movies, and I was ready to believe he was "the Max Perkins of the 1960s." I asked my new friend one favor. "If the book isn't happening, as you call it, please let me know so I can write it off as a tax loss." As I left his office that happy day, I noticed that he withdrew a mysterious file folder from his drawer.

That set my mind whirling. When you write a magazine article, that's the end of the experience. You may get sued occasionally for libel, but nothing really exciting ever happens. The thrill of book publishing is that things can happen and most of them mean extra money.

During the summer of 1965, I sat around the plastic swimming pool on my lawn in Leonia, New Jersey, thinking about who would play the role of me in the movie based on my book. My first choice was Otto Preminger, since that might encourage him to bid for the movie rights. I knew my book lacked characters, plot, subplot and motivation. Yet there were many cases of Hollywood buying books just for the title. "We loved your story, but—" I'm sure the producers told Helen Gurley Brown when they showed her the screenplay for *Sex and the Single Girl*.

I also stopped talking to my old friends, except for the ones who were lawyers, accountants, agents, book reviewers, columnists, television interviewers or underground-film makers.

*The Number One Best Seller* was scheduled to be published in January. My editor told me that I was lucky the date had been postponed; the trade had to be alerted for a book like mine. It was rescheduled for February. The postponement saved my book from certain disaster because Dial now had time to give it the proper build-up in mass media. I was able to thank my lucky stars that the book didn't come out in April, as planned, so the word-of-mouth could get going. When the book finally came out on May 23, I assumed that Dial had rushed it out right in time for the summer slump.

All my editors had been saying about the president of Dial Press, Richard Baron, if there's anything he knows it's how to sell books. Like every innocent, naïve author, I started each day by telephoning his office to find out how my book was doing. "It's *The Number One Best Seller*," he or his secretary assured me. But when I ran into him in Dial's editorial rooms on Third Avenue, he acted as if he had forgotten something important. "What are we going to do with your book?" he asked.

"As a start, we might advertise," I suggested.

I had touched a sore point. Apparently Dial was having trouble with its agency, Sussman & Sugar, over my account. The agency couldn't think of anything to say about my book. "How about something like 'You've read the articles —now read the book.'" I recommended.

Publication day is a major event for an author. Early that morning I rushed out to read *The New York Times* and was shocked to see that my book wasn't reviewed by Eliot Fremont-Smith. It wasn't even listed in "Books Published Today." Being a sensitive nonfiction writer, I was also a little hurt that Dial had decided to omit the usual prepublication party in my honor. These things are of psychological value, and I felt that I needed more of a boost than Roderick Thorp, the other Dial author being published the same week. After all, his book, *The Detective*, had already been bought by the movies and the Literary Guild. His party was at the Regency.

My editor still had not told me the book wasn't happening, as he promised. And there was word-of-mouth, a key publishing index of trends. Everywhere I went—at literary cocktail parties, rental libraries and book stores— people were discussing the number one best seller. Sometimes they got the name of the author wrong, but that was because the full weight of Dial's publicity hadn't been felt.

Puzzled by the fact that copies of *The Number One Best Seller* were not in book stores either, I called a friend who had had three books published and knew the business. "What can I reasonably expect my publisher to do to help my book sell?" I asked.

"Nothing," he said.

He had certainly been right so far. You can imagine how depressed and vulnerable to suggestion I was the night my literary set gathered to celebrate what they still felt was a major literary event. They assured me I was as good a writer as Jackie Susann. "What a shame you're not married to Irving Mansfield," said one well-wisher.

Irving Mansfield is the producer–press agent who seemed to do nothing but push his wife's book in 1966. I rushed to my publisher's defense by pointing out that I had finally been booked to appear on my first TV show, a late-afternoon spot on WNYC-TV. My friends were still enraged by the injustice of it all, and before I knew what was happening I had thirteen Irvings pushing my book.

The Irving who worked for *The New Yorker* said I wouldn't get anywhere in publishing until I invented a new literary art form. "Truman Capote invented the nonfiction novel," he explained. "I've read your book, and what you've done is invented something called 'nonfiction autobiography.' "

My advisers decided to rent Town Hall so that I could announce the new art form to the literary world. I wasn't sure what this had to do with publishing, but like every creative person I've always wanted to make my debut at Town Hall.

Irving the lawyer called the Town Hall management the next morning and asked how much it would cost. "Six hundred dollars," the manager said.

"What hours will the box office be open?"

"The box office is extra. Thirty-five dollars."

"The tickets should read 'Kitman Reads Kitman.'"

"You want tickets, too? That will cost you forty dollars."

"When can *our* artist put up *his* poster in front of the hall?"

"Why didn't you say you wanted to rent space for a poster. Add fifteen dollars more."

Then Irving the lawyer and the manager discussed some of the other details about the reading. "Oh, you want lights on that night," the manager explained. "That's an extra twenty-five dollars." There were also charges for opening the doors to let the crowds in, unlocking the ladies' and men's room doors and other incidentals which brought the bill to $1,300.

Since Capote had read from his works a week earlier for the benefit of the Hampton Boys School, the sponsors hoped the same literary-charity crowd would be deeply interested in helping Ukrainian boys. The Library Fund of the Ukrainian Academy of Arts & Sciences in the U.S., Inc., my favorite charity, had been selected as the beneficiary of the reading.

Actually, the sponsors only hoped to raise enough money to buy a copy of *The Number One Best Seller* for the library, the librarian

**121**

having indicated that the book was not on her spring list. In that sense my debut at Town Hall was a failure, but it was a *succès d'estime.* As a reviewer from *Newsday,* Mike McGrady, wrote:

" 'Nonfictional autobiography means,' Kitman explained to a hushed audience (of two hundred), 'it's the true story of a person writing about himself in depth. Something like this has never been done before.'

"He then briefly discussed his working methods. 'I had a court reporter's machine, a few notebooks, and a secretary or two, and, if you must know, a tape recorder. You can always recognize me at a press conference. I'm the one reporter you can hear saying, 'Did you get that, dear?'

" 'My only problem, I discovered while trying to perfect my memory, was that I couldn't remember the questions any more . . .'

"And then Kitman got to the heart of the matter. 'One of my purposes here,' he said, 'is to read incessantly from my work.' "

I spent the next day checking bookstores, a common workday for authors who have just had books published. Several stores were sold out, I thought, until I found out that they had not received any copies. A store on Fifth Avenue really had been sold out. Both copies of my book had been sold.

Irving the *New York Times* reporter suggested I write to Vincent Gillen, the private detective who had been hired by GM to promote Ralph Nader's book. "The person I want followed is somebody named 'Marvin Kitman.' He is a tall (5'10"), dark, and handsome writer in his mid-thirties. Could you please tell me how much you charge for your editorial services by the day and week. P.S. I would also like to know your rates for only speaking to the press. It would be worth while if you simply implied you were working for somebody important on the case."

Gillen proved to be a great patron of the arts. "If you could furnish the color of each eye," his letter of acceptance read, "the distance between the nostrils and lower lip (use the metric system), and any unusual characteristics such as extra fingers or heads . . ."

Meanwhile, back at the bookstores, whenever people asked for *The Number One Best Seller*, the clerks were still handing them *Valley of the Dolls* and *Human Sexual Response*. I was getting discouraged, but I still hadn't heard anything negative from my editor.

Irving the politician said the problem was my book had not been denounced yet by anybody in Washington. "You're a veteran," he explained. "Why don't you throw your weight around at the Pentagon?" I wasn't sure what it had to do with publishing, but I spoke out on Vietnam anyway:

DISTURBED TO HEAR REPORTS DEFENSE DEPARTMENT WEIGHING ESCALATION OF VIETNAM PEACE EFFORT. AS LARGEST BONDHOLDER IN HUKUANG RAILWAYS IN BERGEN COUNTY, HOPE NO TRUTH TO RUMOR PLANNING BOMB OUR RAILROAD'S PROPERTY ON CHINESE MAINLAND. PLEASE DENY. MARVIN KITMAN PFC (RET). JS51284531.

And then I finally got the kind of literary recognition every writer wants. The United States government revealed it was planning to investigate me. What a lucky break!

Frankly, I didn't know it was a lucky break

**123**

that the Internal Revenue Service had decided to audit my tax forms for 1963–64 until one of my advisers explained it to me. "This is a clear case of harassment," Irving the politician said.

It did seem more than merely coincidence that the IRS should be interested in seeing my books for the first time in my life—immediately after the publication of a book which poked innocent fun at some of the nation's most sacred institutions, like the U.S. Treasury Department. Could they also believe that I was headed for the high tax brackets now that I had a book *almost* in the stores? "If you had won the presidency in 1964," Irving explained, "they wouldn't be investigating you now. You would have put everything in your wife's name."

This is not the proper place to tell the whole story of what happened during the investigation—I'm planning to write a piece for the *Harvard Business Review*—but here is an excerpt from one of the newspaper stories:

"When the Internal Revenue agent showed up for what he assumed would be an average audit of an average taxpayers' return, he was greeted by a battery of reporters, photographers and microphones. And by Marvin Kitman reading a prepared statement.

" 'I welcome this investigation,' he said, 'I have nothing to hide. I fear no public scrutiny. I believe in the public's right to know.'

" 'Have you ever been investigated before?' the tax man asked.

" 'I refuse to answer,' he replied, 'on the grounds that it might tend to incriminate me.' "

What was my publisher doing while I was

winning headlines? Dial Press was going out of business. At least bookstores were not getting copies of my book to sell any more. I finally called my friend, the editor, and asked him what was going on.

He had stopped answering the phone. His secretary said he was busy. "Dial is also publishing other books in 1966," she said.

I knew what she was trying to tell me. "Everybody knows an author's first book doesn't sell," I said, trying to cheer her up. "And my book is right on schedule. I wouldn't be surprised if it's more than fulfilling Dial's expectations, judging by the way they've pushed it. But can't Ed and I still be friends?"

Apparently not. The next communication I received from him was addressed to "Martin Kitman."

Through other sources I learned something about my editor's private life. The mysterious file folder he had been hiding every time I entered his office contained the galleys of his second novel, *Big as Life*, which *his publisher*, Simon and Schuster, had published in May with far less shrift than my book got at Dial. If that's possible.

Maybe it's not such a good idea, Leonard Baker, for a doctor to examine his own broken heart.

# IF I WERE A NETWORK
# PRESIDENT

*Bedtime
Story*

When the editor of *The New Leader* suggested I become its television critic, I declined the honor. It wasn't only that the critics of the other, more important, arts would look down on me. Or that the job lacked security. The truth is I hadn't watched a TV program in years.

The depth of my qualifications immediately made the editor double his proposed honorarium. "Where did you get the notion you'd be expected to *watch* TV programs?" he asked. "That's for the square critics. The medium is the message."

I lack commitment, I went on, listing my shortcomings. I don't hate the networks with a passion. I'm not even sure the programs are bad. My kids never complain about them. "Why don't you watch one program," he said, "and call me back."

I asked my eight-year-old daughter which shoot-'em-up, cowboy or private-eye thriller I should watch. "All the kids are watching *Bravo, Picasso* on NBC tonight," she recommended. "Would you like to see it on my set?" Because of her interest in art—she's one of the best drawers in her grade—I was sure she would be a big help in interpreting Picasso after the Rose Period.

The paintings, drawings, ceramics and sculptures in the Picasso exhibits in Paris and the Dallas/Fort Worth museums came across beautifully on the transatlantic television special. *Bravos* and a few *olés* filled the room time after time. But my daughter was puzzled by Yves Montand's narration. Why did NBC hire an actor who couldn't speak English to introduce the work of a great artist? During the first commercial break, I dug out a book review from a 1950 Paris edition of the *New York Herald Tribune* which explained why Frenchmen like M. Montand speak that way.

Georges Guilaine, in his book titled *La Langue Anglaise en 30 Leçons*—published at about the time Montand was learning English to make his debut in Hollywood—tells his students "How is your mother?" is pronounced "Haouz iz your mozeur?" "But ziz is é minor ponte," I told my daughter. "Lizzaine tou ouot ze man zezz, not tou haou e zezz eet." I realized that was a mistake as soon as Montand went into a technical analysis of Picasso's art.

"What is a mistress?" asked my daughter.

"It's like a fiancée," I explained. A picture of a naked mistress suddenly flashed on the screen. I turned away and made a cutting motion with a finger across the throat, which my wife was supposed to interpret as "Get this child out of here." But she missed her cue.

"Does a model have to be engaged to an artist before she takes off her clothes?"

I looked at my watch. It was only 6:50 P.M. Millions of American children were still awake and at their TV sets. "How could he have two children with somebody he isn't even married to?" my daughter asked.

My God, why aren't they hitting the beep

**127**

button at the network. "What does he mean 'shared his life now with Françoise'?" she asked.

How long has this kind of *cinéma-verité* been going on at NBC? I asked myself. The listing for *Bravo, Picasso* in *TV Guide* didn't say FOR ADULTS ONLY. I remembered what had happened to the moral fiber of Leonia, New Jersey, after Jackie Mason made an adult gesture on the *Ed Sullivan Show*.

"Go to bed," I said firmly. "If you've seen one Picasso you've seen them all."

"But there's going to be an art auction afterward," she said. The moral breakdown was starting already with kids not listening to their fathers. As a compromise, I turned the sound down. "What's a whore of Montmartre?" she asked.

While I was trying to explain the arrondissement system of Paris, Montand blithely admitted that Picasso was a Communist. My daughter asked, "What's communism?"

"It's a terrible economic system, especially for artists. They don't have freedom of expression under communism."

The picture on our screen dissolved to a painting of a women with two noses and three eyes. "In order to be a great artist like Picasso," asked my daughter, "do you have to be a mistress *and* a Communist?" In thirty-seven minutes *Bravo, Picasso* had done more for the cause of communism and free love than all the years of water fluoridation.

Bidding me good night, my daughter said, "Zomeday when ai grow up ai want tou bey a grit artiste laike Pablo Picasso."

That did it. I called up the editor and accepted the job as TV critic. If my daughter ever joins the New Left or lives loosely, I'll sue NBC. Meanwhile, I'm planning to destroy the network as a critic.

---

## Why Critics Hate Television

A network public-relations executive called one day in 1967 to remind me that there was a new television season. "I don't want to influence your opinions," he said, "but I read your reviews last season and I just thought you might want to try something a little different this time by actually watching some of the shows." The official invited me to come into his network's New York skyscraper for a private screening.

If I was going to see one network's new programs, it seemed only fair that I give the others equal time. I found myself scheduled to see the first episodes of twenty-six new series in the next four days, a lot of television for anybody over ten years old.

Although it is a well-known fact that critics don't mean anything in the television business —except in the case of specials and documentaries, where they mean everything—the networks treat friend and foe alike. Since all the critics dislike the programs, it's hard to play favorites. The critic from the Baptist *Messenger* and *The New York Times* democratically are shown the new programs in the same luxurious screening rooms usually reserved for executives, producers and sponsors.

At the CBS Building, for example, a critic can sit in a well-padded swivel chair near the marble coffee table up front, or recline on a divan at the rear of the executive screening room. At NBC, each of the fourteen modern swivel chairs has its own set of dials for controlling the room's lights and sound, as well as two telephones. Presumably these are used when a vice-president has something urgent to say about the programs he has been watching, like "You're fired." The only thing marring my mood of contentment was the fact that the networks hadn't sent a limousine to the suburbs to pick me up.

As my first morning at NBC wore on—I was previewing a Western called *High Chapparal* and a situation comedy, *The Mothers-in-Law*— I suddenly began to realize certain things about the luxurious experience. First, I wasn't a vice president, producer or sponsor. I had come to see TV shows, but curiously there wasn't even a TV set in the room.

"The main cause for disappointment in and for criticism of television," Marshall McLuhan explains in *The Medium Is the Massage*, "is the failure on the part of its critics to view it as a totally new technology which demands different sensory responses. These critics insist on regarding television as merely a degraded form of print technology."

In practice, I discovered that morning, critics actually see technicolor movies on a big screen. It was very interesting seeing the new programs this way, but it seemed to bear little relevance to what my readers would be seeing at home. I was disappointed.

"Is there anything wrong?" asked the NBC public-relations man who had been assigned to take care of me.

**130**    "Yes," I explained. "The picture is in focus.

And I don't see any ghosts on your screen." But I soon had another reason to be disappointed.

During the first pause for a brief message from the sponsor—"INSERT COMMERCIAL HERE" flashed on the big screen—I started to walk out of the room to get something to eat. The film, however, went back on immediately. In four days of screenings, I didn't get a bite to eat.

"Most often the few seconds sandwiched between the hours of viewing—the commericals —reflect a truer understanding of the medium," Marshall McLuhan wrote of the importance of commericals. My old professor at City College, Bernard Rosenberg, said it even better in 1951: "I don't mind the commercials; it's the stuff in between that bothers me." How then is it possible for a critic to judge the overall impact of a program without seeing the most creative aspect of the medium?

Most of my time at the networks was spent in total isolation, an unnatural way to watch television shows. By the second day I couldn't stand the privacy any longer, and invited my wife to join me for a screening of *Cimarron Strip* at CBS. A mix-up occurred. Robert Williams, the *New York Post* TV critic, and his PR shadow were also in the screening room.

"Look at that guy," I whispered, pointing at a bearded man on the screen who had been hiding out in the desert for over a month. "He's out of water, but his teeth are still pearly white. Not even Gleem works that well." Then Stuart Whitman, playing Marshal Jim Crown, began speaking Spanish. (All the Westerns this year are stressing that language, without sub-

**131**

titles, to get a larger share of the ethnic audience.) I asked my wife if she understood what was being said. A teacher in the New York City school system, she began translating: *"Mucho mal hombre* means . . ."

"Shuush," said the PR man, creeping up behind us in the dark, "Bob Williams can't hear."

That actor wasn't speaking pure Shakespeare. If critic Williams had heard less of the dialogue at the screenings, he might not have written in his column a few days later that this is a "gloomy new TV series show season." By arranging private screenings—a kind of lock-in—and preventing a man from even talking to his wife, the networks in effect are forcing a critic to give his total attention to the programs. This is why critics hate television so much, although I don't mean to deprecate other causes such as inept acting, poor direction and incredibly bad writing.

As the hours passed, I found myself working out a reform policy on screenings which would give critics a TV experience *par excellence*, and I pass it on now to the networks at no cost. There should be communal screenings for critics who would sit around the most expensive color TV set money can buy. I would hand each critic a can of beer (or mix him a martini) and a bag of potato chips. During the commercials, the caterers from "21" would run an icebox that would be memorable. I'd also keep a couple of kids in every screening room, beautiful children from Central Casting, who would fight in the background over which programs they wanted to watch.

I was keeping myself occupied like that because of something veteran critic Joan Walker of *Cue* magazine said to me outside the NBC screening room the first morning. She was just finishing up her private study of the 1967–68 season. I asked her if there were any special problems connected with seeing so many new shows, now that the era of the half-hour program was over (The premiere episode of *Cimarron Strip* ran ninety minutes; *High Chapparal* two hours; and ABC's superdocumentary, *Africa*, lasted four hours). "Well, I fall asleep a lot," she confessed.

"What does the responsible critic do in a case like that?"

"I come back and see the programs again. That's what I'm doing here this morning."

With the Labor Day weekend coming up, I decided to keep score of the fatalities. In the four days at the networks, 361 people were killed right before my eyes. These included 67 Apaches, 43 Sioux, 19 half-breeds, 12 Mexicans, 28 Nazis, 128 assorted bushwackers, bank robbers and cattle rustlers. The gringos also suffered heavy losses. The U.S. 7th Cavalry Regiment lost 21. Three Marshall's deputies died (I learned from *Cimarron Strip* they were paid only one dollar a day, so that didn't reduce the Federal budget much). Four white women were killed, and 11 cowboys were wrapped in white linen.

I know this makes the 1967–68 season sound like a violent one. But spread out over two weeks—the premiere period—all that gore may not be so noticeable.

It really isn't fair to judge a series by its first episode. The producers spend a lot of extra money on the first show, which is often the pilot aimed at a very small audience consisting of two people: the network vice president in charge of programming and the sponsor. Suffice it to say for the moment that it really is "A Very Special Season" (as ABC's advertising calls it), "The Year of Event Television" (NBC), and "In the Winner's Circle" (CBS).

For the first time you will be able to see an adventure story about an Indian boy whose mother is an elephant (NBC's *Maya*), a great improvement over that poor fellow whose mother was a car; a situation comedy about a flying nun (ABC's *The Flying Nun*); a crime show whose hero is a detective in a wheelchair (NBC's *Ironsides*); and a Western based on the life of General George Armstrong Custer (ABC's *Custer*), which finally explains what the Association on American Indian Affairs means by its bumper sticker CUSTER DIED FOR YOUR SINS.

All of these shows, I'm sure, will run for five years—except *Custer*. Everybody knows he will get massacred.

---

*Kitman's First Law*

Somehow I seem to have lost all the notes I took while screening the first episodes of the new television season's twenty-six new series. My first reaction to this awful discovery was to ask the networks to show me all twenty-six again to refresh my memory. But fortunately I found I hadn't been able to forget those programs; some nights I can't even sleep thinking about them.

I worry, for example, about that poor nun over at ABC who flies. I can't bear the thought of a young novice flying alone out there every Thursday night without instruments. Although I still turn a button three times whenever I see a nun, I'm not a religious man. Yet I was very moved by the performance of Sally Fields (Gidget in the series of the same name, before she turned to religion) as Sister Bertrille, the first teeny-bopper at the Convent San Tanco in San Juan, Puerto Rico.

"Of all the flying nuns I've seen," read one of my lost notes, "she is probably the most likable." Miss Fields is a real swinger who plays gin rummy, dances the frug, is strong on civil rights (she has served time in jail, one of the sisters remarks, for her part in a free-speech protest) and knows aerodynamics. "I'm light," she explained in the first episode of *The Flying Nun* to all the doubting Saint Thomases, "and when the wind is right—I fly." Everybody who has ever flown recognizes this as a version of the lift-plus-thrust, load-plus-drag principle.

To some of the critics, she seems to be the child of a marriage between *Mary Poppins* and *The Sound of Music*. But she reminds me most of Saint-Exupéry, missing in flight since 1944.

There was a note on my pad to interview Harry Ackerman, the executive producer who, I believe, came up with the idea for *The Flying Nun*, and ask him if he believed in transmogrification—which might explain what I feel is the uncanny resemblance to the French aviator and author. Since this is probably the most inspired and best show of the new season, I also wanted to ask if he was working on a spin-off, perhaps something about a rabbinical student who could walk on water. But it's just as well that I lost the note. I wouldn't want to be in the same room with Ackerman: he's going to get hit by lightning some day.

Other nights I worry about what television is doing to poor Walter Brennan, who, as Jack Gould correctly pointed out in *The New York Times*, plays Walter Brennan in *The Guns of Will Sonnett*. The beloved star of *The Real McCoys* kills three men in the first episode of his new ABC Western. "Revenge is like a sore," he explains to his grandson after the gun battle, "that don't never heal." I knowed he had to kill them men: they was gunning for him. But I'm worried about Walter Brennan anyway.

I also toss at night thinking about the anti-Vietnam propaganda the doves out in Hollywood are slipping into our Westerns. For example, there is Leif Erickson, the Arizona cattle baron in NBC's *High Chaparral*, telling us how much he wants to live in peace and brotherhood with the Apaches. "They are a people fighting for their homeland," he explains only a few minutes before he slaughters the Indian nationalists. Erickson looks and rides like Barry Goldwater, but he sounds like President Johnson.

Mostly, though, what keeps me up at night is trying to understand what the networks had in mind when they spent millions to create this particular set of twenty-six shows. I don't mean to imply that this isn't a *successful* season in the sense that the French critic Boileau used the word. After reading a sonnet submitted to him by Louis XIV, M. Boileau is said (by Irving Babbitt in *Masters of Modern French Criticism*) to have remarked: "Sire, nothing is impossible for your Majesty. You set out to write some bad verses, and you have succeeded."

It is inconceivable that three competing networks, working independently in complete secrecy, could produce by accident twenty-six new series so similar in quality. There has to be a master plan, a new approach to programming, which we critics just don't understand.

In the past the networks have produced drivel. This year in their regular programming they have gone in heavily for *pure drivel*. There is a big difference, as those of us who watch and love television know.

I have a hunch that the networks really are trying to kill television once and for all. Not all of it, just the classic art forms—the Westerns, situation comedies and crime shows. Let this be Kitman's Law: *Pure drivel tends to drive off the screen ordinary drivel.*

There is an ominous note in the network publicity departments' restrained praise for this season. It's so quiet you can almost hear an option drop. When the new shows die, the networks will rush to substitute highbrow programming, movies like *Mutiny on the Bounty*. The drive to turn our television sets into neighborhood movies—called "diversified programming"—is an alarming trend. But I have finally figured out a way everybody can enjoy the current programs, and thus thwart the networks' evil scheme.

Mainly you have to ignore the conventional program categories. (The networks, by the way, are already doing this: They call their new movies "specials.") One reason NBC's *The*

*Mothers-in-Law* is such a disappointment is that it is identified as a "situation comedy." The average viewer immediately has a chip on his shoulder: All right, he thinks, make me laugh. Well, that's been a hard thing to do since the Red Chinese got the hydrogen bomb.

However, if you think of the Eve Arden–Kaye Ballard show—it's about a couple of nice kids in love who have these two impossible mothers—as a soap opera, which it really is, *The Mothers-in-Law* immediately strikes you as very amusing and sophisticated. The same is true, incidentally, of CBS's *He and She*, the story of a rich cartoonist who is trying to get richer. To further enhance your enjoyment of the new soap operas, every time you hear canned laughter substitute in your mind the sound of an organ.

Don't throw away the canned laughter, though. Simply insert it in the Westerns. One of the funniest situation comedies I've seen in years is *Custer*. I guess you could call the genre "red humor," for it ultimately turns the Indians into good guys and the U.S. Army into bad guys. That is a laugh; it is also a one-sided interpretation of history. Historians have been laughing at Westerns for years, but I recommend this one for laymen as well. One warning: it's habit-forming.

I have watched four episodes of *Custer* so far, I'm ashamed to say, and now find myself looking forward to Wednesday nights the way I used to get hung up on *The Long Ranger*. Part of my devotion to this ABC show, I admit, is morbid curiosity. I want to see how it ends.

These first few weeks the writers have been

sketching in the character of the man who at twenty-four, during the Civil War, was the youngest general in the U.S. Army. We meet him now as a lieutenant colonel during the postwar period. Custer gives the impression of being a relatively simply-minded soldier who only wants to kill Indians. His motives actually are more complex: He is an ambitious career officer and kills Indians because it is the fastest way to get ahead in the military establishment of the 1870s, just as killing Vietcong is a steppingstone in Vietnam today. "I started at the top," he reminisces in one episode, "and I'm working my way down."

It's easy to see why things haven't been breaking right for Lieutenant Colonel Custer. He is insubordinate. In every episode, he disobeys an order. How he gets away with it is the plot. I've been making my kids watch each installment with me to show them what eventually happens to people who don't follow orders.

The bad guys—Wayne Maunder as the boy ex-general, and Slim Pickens, who was Major King Kong in the movie *Dr. Strangelove* and now plays the boy's scout—are comic figures. Maunder studied acting with Stella Adler and rides like Tom Mix. Seeing him in action reminded me of Robert Sherwood's remark about Mix in the old *Life*: "They say he rides like a part of the horse, but they don't say which part." He is funny from the moment he rides into Fort Hays, Kansas, in the first episode, his long golden curls flowing, and proceeds to beat up the toughest man in the fort without a curl unwinding (canned laughter). When he calls for his dogs, the company clerk brings a pair of matched afghans (canned laughter).

Still, neither Maunder nor Pickens is as funny as Michael Dante, who plays the good guy, Chief Crazy Horse. With his long, straight black hair, Dante doesn't look like an Indian, which makes him something of a sight gag. He is smarter than Custer—the boy soldier, we learn in one episode, ranked thirty-fourth in his class of thirty-four at West Point. And he speaks like one of those Oglala Sioux who has been to Oxford under a cultural exchange program. His English is pure poetry:

> *Yellow Hair is a tree*
> *In the wind.*
> *He will bend.*
> *Then break.*

There probably won't be more dialogue like Chief Crazy Horse's on television until the networks try a fictionalized historical treatment of the life of Mao Tse-tung.

Thus far, Custer has managed to escape from every trap set by Crazy Horse. "There will be other days, Yellow Hair," the Indian cries to the heavens in the fourth episode. And we believe him. *Custer* has been doing poorly in the early Nielsens, but ABC could beef up the ratings and perform a public service at the same time by advertising the last show of the series—which can't be too many moons away —as a "special." As they said when the crowds turned up at the funeral of Columbia Pictures president Harry Cohn in Hollywood, "You give the people what they want, and they'll come out."

I feel I owe an apology to anyone who followed my recommendations and watched the programs I praised so highly in my review of the new television season. In my zeal to cover the season thoroughly, I forgot to mention a most important point: The programs will seem quite boring unless you tune in after they have been under way for a while.

Just how much of a program should be missed before it begins to seem interesting is a controversy I wouldn't want to get involved in. However, I cannot stress too strongly the importance of missing the part where the writer explains what his story is all about.

The plot, as it is sometimes called, may be concealed in the weekly episode's title, in a line of dialogue, or even in an entire scene. So it's pointless to arbitrarily suggest you miss, say, the first four minutes of a lawyer show like ABC's *Judd* or the first twenty-nine minutes of the adventure program *Gentle Ben* on CBS. You just have to use the hit-or-miss technique until you get your timing. It's worth the extra effort.

Why the average program is improved by lack of knowledge of who did what, I'm not sure. It simply happens to be the kind of mystery which can sustain *any* program, whatever its shortcomings of script, acting or direction. My law on this matter is as follows: *The whole of a program is never equal to its parts.* Despite their different programming philosophies, this rule applies to all three networks.

As sound as my advice and its theoretical underpinning may seem, frankly there are times when even I doubt it helps much. Then

I tune in late on some program and I'm struck dumb anew by how well it works in practice.

The fifth episode of *Custer* may have bored some people to death. But barging in late, I found myself an eyewitness to an amazing historical *shtick*. For some reason Yellow Hair, to use Lieutenant Colonel Custer's Indian name, was fighting side by side with Chief Crazy Horse. Just the week before the Sioux leader had sworn to kill Yellow Hair. He had made the same threat a week earlier. Yet now they had formed a popular front and were slinging lead at unidentified redmen and whitemen. It was the first machination in the plot since the series began in September. For most of the hour the two brave warriors shot at everything that moved, regardless of race, color or creed. It warmed my heart to find the races could work together on something.

Before I found out why the two men had buried the hatchet, I received an even more startling history lesson: at one point Yellow Hair saved Crazy Horse's life. He apparently felt the need to justify this action. "There is talk," Custer said between clenched teeth, "that you have white blood in you, Crazy Horse." Students of American history will recognize this as the 1870s way of saying, "That's funny, you don't look like an Indian."

Custer did not reveal the source of his inside information; presumably it came from the 7th Cavalry's G-2. But Crazy Horse went white with rage. "Yellow Hair," he snarled, "don't you ever say anything like that again." Crazy Horse stared hard at Yellow Hair's long golden curls, and I would not have been surprised if he had scalped him on the spot. But that would have been historically inaccurate.

A backlash of the premise at the forty-seven-minute mark eventually gave away the secret of what this show was all about. But the momentum of my confusion carried me through.

I felt especially bad about not mentioning sooner this wonderful device for improving programs when I heard the depressing news that *Custer* is scheduled to bite the dust in January. According to my records, this is the third month in a row I have praised the program. A critic less certain of his judgment might feel this reflected on his lack of power with the networks. But I see it as yet another case of the networks' bowing to outside pressures. The Red Power movement hates *Custer* and has been lobbying vigorously for its death.

Less understandable is ABC's decision to kill at the same time a show called *Good Company*. As far as I can see, the only reason ABC is down on F. Lee Bailey's interview show is his low Nielsen rating. *Good Company* is eighty-first, or last, but everybody knows the Nielsens are inaccurate. This show deserved to be eightieth.

I had not written about lawyer Bailey's debut in show business for fear of influencing the jury while he was on trial. Now that the verdict is in, I would like to comment on the injustice of it all.

The idea of reviving the person-to-person concept with Bailey in Ed Murrow's role came out of that hotbed of creative thinking in television today, David Susskind's Talent Associ-

**143**

ates. This was the shop which also gave us *N.Y.P.D.* this season, the first police show to base its stories on the files of the New York Police Department—a marked departure from the classic police show, which usually uses the files of the Los Angeles Police Department.

When I first learned about Bailey's going on television, I feared for him. Being untrained in the law, I read Martin Mayer's book, *The Lawyers*. That told me more than I wanted to know about the profession, including Canon 27 of the Canons of Professional Ethics adopted by the American Bar Association. It states:

It is unprofessional to solicit professional employment by circulars, advertisements, through touters or by personal communications or interviews not warranted by personal relations. Indirect advertisements for professional employment such as furnishing or inspiring newspaper comments, or producing his photograph to be published in connection with causes in which the lawyer has been or is engaged or concerning the manner of their conduct, the magnitude of the interest involved, the importance of the lawyer's position, and all other like self-laudation, offend the traditions and lower the tone of our profession and are reprehensible.

I didn't fully understand that canon, but was afraid the American Bar Association might think the show was nothing but a multi-dollar advertisement for Bailey's talents as an attorney. After seeing him in action for several weeks, though, my concern is that he will go bankrupt as a lawyer.

The series began with Bailey cross-examining actor Tony Curtis at his home in Beverly Hills. "Hello," said America's most famous criminal lawyer as he stepped out of his convertible in the Curtis driveway. "We're going to see what they're really like," he explained of the line of questioning to be pursued with the celebrities. "We think they're good company."

The opening sequence was memorable because it finally gave Curtis the opportunity to speak his mind on art. "This is what you call a hard-edge painting," Curtis elaborated about a work by a French artist named Levy. "It means something, at least to me."

We also discovered that Curtis is an artist himself. "I make boxes," he admitted, showing several of them while confiding he was inspired by the American box maker Joseph Connell. "It will be difficult to explain the essence of what I mean with the boxes," he added.

Curtis spoke about a lot of things, including the definition of success ("It means doing better than your best friend"), but he kept coming back to his passion for boxes. Knowing Curtis's reputation as a comedian, I couldn't help feeling there was a private joke in there somewhere that Bailey had missed.

*Good Company* did not hit its stride until the interview with Hugh Hefner at his Chicago mansion. I wrote down some of the exchange because I had never heard anything like it:

Q. Is this your bar, Hugh?

A. Yes, Lee, this is my bar.

Q. You really seem to have a lot of liquor here, Hugh.

A. Yes, Lee, I have a lot of liquor here.

Q. How many bars like this do you have around your house, Hugh?

A. Three, Lee.

**145**

Q. Are they all stocked with liquor like this one, Hugh?

A. Yes, Lee, just like this.

Q. Why do you keep so much liquor around, Hugh?

A. Well, people come to the house, Lee, and they like a drink.

Q. You mean you're a good host, Hugh?

A. Yes, Lee, I'm a good host.

Q. Say, Hugh, this is a terrific swimming pool.

A. Yes, Lee, it is a terrific swimming pool.

Naturally, there's more to *Good Company* than stimulating conversation. For example, Hefner asked Bailey during the tour of the *Playboy* publisher's famous bedroom, "Would you like a ride on my bed, Lee?"

"Yes, I would like a ride," answered the great criminal lawyer. And around they went on the motorized bed.

The next time I murder anyone, I will certainly think twice about hiring F. Lee Bailey as counsel. But there is still time for him to save his career. All he has to do is act like a lawyer. I don't mean asking nasty questions like, "Where were you on the night of . . . ?" When a celebrity says, "Now you just sit here a minute while I go bring in my wife and children," Bailey should open up a drawer or two and rifle the contents.

Summers have been occurring on television since David Sarnoff officially launched the industry at the New York World's Fair in 1939. But summer seems to set in earlier than usual every year. *The Jackie Gleason Show* went to reruns on February 17 (1968). In the fortnight beginning March 15 alone, 12 network programs knocked off for the season. These included one of my nominees for an Emmy award —for the most creative use of film on a TV show—NBC's *Tuesday Night at the Movies*.

It is currently fashionable to attack the industry for cutting the regular season; a "year" for a typical series these days lasts twenty-six weeks. Well, I remember the old days when the television summer began in June—but not fondly. The seasons really dragged then.

A harbinger of summer is the critics' denunciation of reruns. Some critics don't even watch television during the summer, on the theory that the shows they disliked the first time will hardly have improved with age. This is the same as saying there would be no value in the critics' repeating their September-February reviews.

Yet the rerun season, it has always seemed to me, does not have to be a summer of discontent. It could be a time for experimentation. For instance, one might view summer programming as a retrospective, a kind of festival of what the industry considers the best shows produced in the heyday of TV—that golden age of three or four months ago.

Along with millions of other people, I have been watching this exhibition for several weeks now. I have seen dozens of classics representing the flowering of thirty years of

**147**

creativity in the medium—everything from specials, old movies and Westerns to crime, talk, variety, situation and topical comedy shows. It wasn't a complete waste of time, for I have been able to formulate a new law on televison: *If it moves, the public will watch it.*

Still, there is something to be said for the TV summer season: it keeps a lot of people off the streets at night. Whatever the programs' shortcomings as art, they are unquestionably more cheerful to watch than the spectacle of our cities going up in smoke.

It was disappointing to see that the educational television station in New Jersey (Channel 13) has not similarly taken advantage of the lull before the winter of discontent sets in to put on a festival of the best of last season's Public Broadcast Laboratory shows. My ideas about the nature of experimental television have changed radically since the debut of the Public Broadcast Laboratory in 1967. Actually this isn't as great an accomplishment for PBL as it might seem. My ideas on the subject were quite vague.

Such a look backward at the series of experiments in broadcasting would not necessarily be entertaining, but it would be educational. There isn't a better way to see where the PBL and Ford Foundation people went wrong than by watching the best of their shows. A discovery like this would be especially timely today in the light of early reports on what the Corporation for Public Broadcasting is planning for us in the field of noncommercial TV.

There is no official connection between PBL, the founding father of experimental broadcasting as we know it, and CPB, the brainchild of the forces for good television in Congress. What they have in common is a passion for experimentation. In the public mind, however, CPB undoubtedly will become known as the Son of PBL. And it is in the public interest that CPB doesn't become one of those sons who never profit from the mistakes of the father.

It always hurt to see the Ford Foundation waste its hard-earned money in broadcasting, especially when there are still so many other areas in which the foundation could relentlessly try to improve the quality of American life. One area of basic research I wish they would get into in a big way is the search for a new car that will last as long as a 1948 Oldsmobile. The money CPB is in the process of wasting is the taxpayers'. So I have a financial, as well as an artistic, stake in being concerned that history doesn't repeat itself, like one of those glasses of beer we are always seeing on commercial television.

When PBL began its noble experiments, what Fred Friendly, McGeorge Bundy and Av Westin had in mind was to give the public a meaningful alternative to commercial television. To make this dream come true, PBL hired experienced, gifted network personnel, who were then turned loose to do all the things they've ever wanted to do in the medium, without having to worry about sponsors, network vice presidents or, for that matter, the public.

Any list of PBL's accomplishments in the two years it lived would have to include such innovations as having a number of people talking at the same time on camera. These production numbers, with from two to forty-seven participants, had never been tried on television before, for good reason. You couldn't hear what anybody was saying during the confrontations.

Then there was the experimental notion of giving controversial news stories, like the race issue, one-sided treatment. It seemed to me at the time this technique was introduced in the first PBL show in the fall of 1967 that the lab would never be able to equal the network news staffs in this department.

And who will ever forget that "provocative experiment in nationwide Public Television," as the PBL newspaper ads described the third show, which consisted of an interview with Walter Lippmann? I've never met the man personally, yet I feel I know Walter Lippmann a little, having watched him being interviewed in depth seven times on CBS in recent years. It's always a pleasure seeing good old Walt again. The wrinkle this time was the shallowness of the questions asked by well-meaning, but not especially well informed, college journalists. A jealous thought crossed my mind. If I were on a $10-million grant from the Ford Foundation, it ran, I bet I could have come up with an interview idea like that.

Somehow all of this wasn't enough to justify the effort and money that went into this alternative to commercial television. A new dimension had not been added.

The major thrust of PBL's experiments, it is now clear, was in the areas of public affairs and news. The only problem with this direction was that, whatever the networks' other flaws, these happen to be the areas where they do their best work.

It is easy now to understand PBL's predilection. Westin and Friendly both came from the public-affairs and news areas of broadcasting (CBS). It was natural that they were obsessed with correcting the blemishes in the networks' coverage, which turned out to be not readily discernible to the average eye.

What are the areas of expertise in the backgrounds of the new experimenters at CPB? Without singling out any individuals for praise, it probably can be said safely that they know how to communicate effectively with Congress. There is also a wealth of educational television station management talent.

Some PBL veterans who had to "sell" their so-called experiments to the ETV managers every week are not wild about this qualification. "They always used to say, 'Give us Yves Montand,'" recalls one producer-in-exile. "I remember showing a station manager a six-year-old film of Yves Montand doing Yves Montand, produced by French television in the avant-garde style pioneered by the Andy Williams variety show. He was very excited about it. He said, 'Now you fellows are finally getting somewhere.'"

The experiments in public broadcasting the CPB board of directors have announced thus far have one element in common: they are all underfunded. This is not always the road to excellence in programming. WMVS in Milwaukee has been given the challenge "to commission and produce a color-television ballet to be danced and filmed on spectacular wilderness locations around the state," according to the CPB press release, on fifteen thousand dollars. WITF in Hershey, Pennsylvania, received

**151**

$49,980 to make *three* ninety-minute color programs on a rather large subject: exploring man's control of man, taping mixed-media encounters, combining film dramatization, live psychodrama and audience confrontation and interreaction, on "The Loss of Privacy," "The Limits of Dissent" and "The Control of Life."

"They won't be able to light up the studios with that kind of money," one film maker explained. A lean budget for a documentary should include approximately a thousand dollars a minute for studio costs. Hopefully, a station like WMVS will be able to cut traditional costs by using Brownie cameras. But one shudders to think about the travel expenses involved in locating wilderness "spectacular" enough for some of those temperamental ballerinas.

What is more disturbing about the list of CPB grants is the subject matter of the programs. A New Orleans television station has been given inadequate funds to make five half-hours on the Acadian way of life in Louisiana. A St. Paul station has been commissioned to make three hour-long programs telling the history of the revolutionary populist movements in the upper Midwest. A Maine station is doing three half-hour programs on the dry subject of Maine humor.

CPB's basic orientation seems suspiciously like PBL's obsession with public affairs and news. Even worse, it sounds like Charles Kuralt's travel schedule for next fall. Not that there is anything wrong with Kuralt's on-the-road shows for CBS.

Why should taxpayers' money go down the drain with more documentaries when there are so many other depressed areas in broadcasting which have been ignored too long? My theory is that the things in between the news and public affairs are in much worse shape.

## 2.

Despite the technical brilliance of the networks today, I've always had the recurring fantasy that I could do a fairly good job running one of them. I would not only date the chorus girls on the variety shows. My real strength as a network president would be in the area of creative programming.

I'm sure that even I would have known that situation comedy shows about widows were going to be hot in 1968–69. I don't know how I would have known it—cynics say it was mere coincidence that Doris Day, Diahann Carroll and Mrs. Muir showed up on the networks as widows—it's just something I feel. If I were a network president today, I'd be out in Hollywood signing up Jane Russell to play an orphan girl. I just feel that situation comedies about orphans will be big next season.

Hardly a night goes by when I don't get an idea for a major breakthrough in television programming. Mostly, these concepts run to public service. The other night, for example, it occurred to me that once a month a responsible network should run the last ten minutes of the previous month's movies in prime time. Old movies were made for viewing in theaters. They usually start off fast, then bog down in the frills of character development. Once they have you in a theater, there's nothing to do but sit there patiently, waiting for the story to

**153**

zoom to its dramatic finish. But watching these pre-TV movies in bed, many viewers fall asleep. You'd be amazed at how many people are walking around wondering how such all-time film greats as *The Vampire and the Girl* ended. A festival of the last ten minutes of all the month's previous movies also would appeal to people who enjoy reading the last three pages of mysteries.

It's hard to sell new ideas like that to sponsors who are set in their ways. Yet the networks have many old formats which have not been used in some time.

Take a new pilot I'm working on called *Person-to-Person*. Instead of dropping in on people like the Lunts—the old Ed Murrow approach—I plan to visit the homes of real people who excite the American public's curiosity, places like Allen Ginsberg's apartment in the East Village. To make the concept even more exciting, I would also add the element of surprise used so well in *Candid Camera* by dropping in at 2 A.M.

As host for this show I would want a genial old man wearing a blue pin-striped suit and a snap-brim hat, somebody like J. Edgar Hoover. Image-wise, the host has to project incorruptibility because the public still remembers the dishonesty of the old Murrow show. There won't be any of that planning months ahead or rehearsing questions and answers.

The new *Person-to-Person* show will open every week with a knock at the door. Host Hoover then presents the occupant with a search warrant. Allen Ginsberg interrupts his chanting of *Hare Krishna* to say, "Hello, Ed.

We've been expecting you to stop by sooner or later. Come right in."

There's a close-up shot of J. Edgar Hoover wiping his palms with a white handkerchief before shaking hands with the poet-religious leader. "Just step over those mattresses on the floor, Ed," Ginsberg says cordially. On a cue from their chief a dozen technicians, also in snap-brim hats, rush into the apartment.

After a brief message from the sponsor, giving the production crew time to set up equipment, the program resumes with the cameras catching the Ginsberg family circle tidying up the apartment for the unexpected guests. Everybody is frantically fanning the smoke or throwing packets out the open windows. In the background there is the sound of toilets being flushed. "Well, this is a nice surprise, Ed," Ginsberg says, offering Hoover a seat. "Make yourself comfortable. Anything special on your mind?"

"No, I'd just like to ask a few questions. What period couch is this, Al?"

"Well, we just call it a mattress, Ed. Can I get you anything to eat, a cube of sugar, a smoke?"

"What's going on in that room, Al?"

"I'm sorry, Ed. I forgot you'd like to look around the pad. That's the kitchen."

"What smells so good?"

"We're baking bananas, Ed. Over here in this room we pray for peace. Would you like to join us, Ed?"

"What's in here, Al?"

"I wouldn't go in there if I were you, Ed. Some of the people are turning on."

**155**

"Tell me, Al, are you married?"

"I'd like you to meet Peter," Ginsberg says proudly, taking the interviewer by the arm and steering him into the music room. "Put down the sitar and finger cymbals, Peter, and shake hands with Ed. He's with *Person-to-Person*. You know we're a mixed marriage, Ed. Peter's a Muslim and I'm a tantric Hindu. My guru was against the match, Ed, but we've been very happy."

For the second week of the new *Person-to-Person* show, we could drop in at the home of Candy Mossler and her nephew in Florida.

If I were a network president, I would also experiment with a new quiz show, called *$640,000 Question*. Contestants are given that amount of money at the beginning of the program. A team of *Time, Ramparts* and *Life* magazine researchers has spent weeks investigating the background of each guest. The host asks ten questions, all of which are very embarrassing. But the contestant doesn't have to answer. He can cry, "I take the Fifth." Each time he takes that way out, however, he loses $64,000 from his pile.

*What's My Drug?*, another private-affairs program, is a little like the old John Daly show CBS dropped a few seasons back, except panelists are medical doctors, pharmacists, trained social workers and narcotics officers. They listen to the mystery guests' symptoms and visions and try to guess which drug he's addicted to. Edward Anslinger would be the host. The show can't miss top ratings if authorities are right about the number of people on drugs today.

**156**  If I were a network president, I wouldn't do

anything about making situation comedies which dealt with real people's problems. That's hopeless. The American audience has to identify with cars that can talk, nuns who can fly and wives who can solve job problems by witchery.

### 3.

These are the normal daydreams of a television critic. I've written about them in the past, but for some reason they never caught on at PBL. The innovators at CPB undoubtedly have their own ideas about how to improve the medium's basic art forms. There is, however, one area nobody in broadcasting ever seems to give any thought to perfecting.

First off, baseball is a game in which so little is happening, you don't really need to telecast all of it. The game should occupy only the top part of the screen. On the bottom part, you could have a ribbon of tape from the Western Union ticker showing all the out-of-town scores and developments. The real fan watches the scoreboard almost as much as he watches the game, so he would get all this information. He'd get more than what the scoreboard gives because the ticker gives home runs, changes of pitchers, etc. It would be just like the stock market reports New York's WOR-TV runs continuously on its screen every afternoon.

Secondly, I would change the announcing setup. Right now, many of the announcers are what you call "house men." They announce the game as if they are talking to the club owner, or even worse, to the players' wives. I understand almost anything remotely critical

**157**

said about a ball player will offend his wife. For example, saying her husband fumbled a ground ball particularly angers a wife as being prejudicial to her man. She says it takes the bread and butter out of their mouths, I hear.

I envision a setup in which you would have three types of announcers on a team. One would be the house man who would cater to the wives and club owners. The second would be the objective reporter concerned only with the "who, what, when, why" we learned about in high school journalism.

The third fellow would be the critic. His job would involve the highest facility of criticism, a sort of H. L. Mencken of the airwaves. He would be a sound baseball man, yet wit and intelligence would not disqualify him. He would revel in errors and poor play. He would poke fun at the athletes at appropriate times, pointing up imperfections, warts and buffooneries.

To keep up his high level of impartiality, he wouldn't travel with the team so he would not become personal friends of the athletes. A guard would be stationed outside the announcer's booth so that irate home fans and players' wives couldn't inflict physical harm upon him. He might be considered revolutionary at first, but once baseball people understood he was only doing his job I'm sure they would understand. I'm sure there are any number of reporters, columnists and ex-baseball people out of favor who could handle this assignment neatly.

To eliminate much of the prattle with which announcers fill dead time, I would substitute live microphones in the dugouts and bullpens.

We would then hear the meaningful comments of the athletes while the game was in progress. Some people might object because we might be exposed to profanity or learn a team's playing secrets. That could be overcome by having a team official screen their remarks. The team official would monitor out all undesired comments the way they do on radio phone-interview shows, and then he would filter the rest through on a delayed tape.

An experiment in baseball broadcasting would have to come to grips with the disturbing trend of the networks' hiring baseball stars as announcers. NBC's *Game of the Week* especially has been guilty of throwing young kids into the announcer's box before they are ready.

Sandy Koufax (the modern Jewish Samson), who made a name for himself as a Los Angeles Dodgers pitcher, is an example of what happens when these kids are exploited by the networks. Although he started out two years ago as a bad monologist, today he is also a poor interviewer. If Koufax had learned the fundamentals of his new profession by working as a bartender, a host in a bowling alley or even as a radio disc jockey, he might have developed a style. In the high-pressure world of network television, Koufax has gone inside himself and become inarticulate.

Tony Kubek, the ex-New York Yankee infielder and another NBC expert-in-residence, goes to the other extreme and talks too much. "Tell me, Mick," he said to NBC's rookie find of 1969, Mickey Mantle, before the San Diego–San Francisco game, "I don't want to make you nervous. But are you nervous?"

The former Yankee outfielder, making his

**159**

debut before the mikes, said, "Yes." He sounded nervous.

Tony filled the dead air with a brief rundown of everything they would be discussing. "I don't think the mounds were ever uniform before," Mick cut in nervously.

"What about the new strike zone, Mick? You know it's now under the armpit to the knees. It used to be from the shoulders to the knees."

"Well, if you ask me, the umpires never followed the old strike zones. Each umpire has his own strike zone."

Instead of wasting Mantle on inane pregame interviews, with the ex-ballplayer's connections, he could be stationed in the locker room for vignettes. "We're in the showers with Lester 'Boom Boom' Lemming, the rookie pitcher who was blasted off the new low mound in the first inning of his first major-league game and has just been handed a bus ticket to Lockport, Pennsylvania. In your opinion, what happened out there today, Boom Boom?"

More than likely Boom Boom Lemming would only say something like, "Well I guess I just didn't have my stuff today, folks." But maybe once a month in an experimental season something very exciting might happen.

Why go to the games when the telecasts would be so much more rewarding?

People don't seem to go to the ball park to watch the games anymore. They go to wave to the television cameras. Well, I would cater to that instinct by showing five solid minutes of crowd action at intervals throughout the game. I would put the crowd scenes on a set schedule; the third-base crowd after the second inning, the people behind first base after the fourth inning, and so on. People then would know what was coming. You wouldn't find people picking their noses or something the way you sometimes do now.

Who knows what might happen if people knew for sure they would be on television at specific times? The parks might be filled every day. I can see a pretty girl being discovered for the movies from having been spotted at the ball park on the television screen. It might be as ripe a proving ground for the movies as Schwab's Drug Store in Hollywood.

It is possible that a major-league team might not want to encourage the growth of television as an art form in this way. But surely there is some minor-league team without a television contract which could see the publicity advantages of participating.

I am not claiming any of these ideas would work in practice. The principle of experimental television is not that the experiment be successful. Public broadcasting has to say, "We're innovators. We may strike out most of the time with our experiments. But when we get a hit, it's a homer." I hope the Corporation for Public Broadcasting isn't just talking a good game.

# PART THREE

# HEROES

## THE GREAT MEN

Every year a handful of writers breaks into television. A case history of one of the lucky few, it occurred to me, might say something about the medium. Harold Robbins, the beginner I picked to study, had his first series, *The Survivors*, starring Lana Turner and George Hamilton, presented on Monday nights from September 1969 to January 1970.

Robbins, I learned the first time I met him, wasn't overly enthusiastic about working for the new medium because of its low creative standards. "All the networks can pay a writer," he explained, "is in the low six figures. I can't do my best work for that kind of money."

We were in Harold's suite at the Plaza Hotel, where he stays on his rare visits to New York to attend to the details of a new TV writer's career, such as the writing. The last time he

*Only You, Harold Robbins*

**163**

flew in from his home on the Riviera in 1968 to do research for what ABC has been calling in its press releases "one of the most ambitious series ever produced for television," there were thirty-nine girls from a famed ballet company in the suite, drinking champagne and dancing on a coffee table in the nude. I missed that opportunity to interview him. But another television critic who was there said it was a waste of time. The ballerinas sat on his note pad.

This time Robbins seemed to be in the mood for a serious discussion about the technical problems of writing for TV for the first time. "Are you worried about compromising your integrity by working for television?" I asked the author of *The Carpetbaggers*, *79 Park Avenue*, and *The Adventurers*.

"I know it must sound that way to those familiar with my work," Robbins said. "For my next movie, *The Inheritors*, I have a deal that guarantees me 3 and ¾."

"3 and ¾ what?" I interrupted.

"Million. I can stay on the air for three years with *The Survivors* and not get that much."

I asked him how he had gotten into this fiscal mess.

"I had lunch a couple of years ago with Leonard Goldenson, the president of ABC," Robbins recalled of how it all started. "I gave him a one-line synopsis of my idea: 'How about a TV series called *The Survivors*?'"

Robbins has always been something of a hero to many writers. What we admire most about him is his sales. The same thing can be said for Admiral Farragut. Robbins also is one of the few writers who can sell his books to publishers for more than a million dollars on the basis of one-page outlines. Still I couldn't believe that hard-nosed network executives would commit themselves to a costly series, by a writer without a track record, with only a sketchy story line. I was right.

"A year later," Robbins confessed, "there was a meeting about the show at ABC headquarters in New York. 'What's it going to be?' the executives asked me point blank. 'We have to know what the story is about.'

"I was curious myself. I hadn't thought it through yet. Everybody had their eyes on me as I walked over to the glass window behind Goldenson's desk. From the thirty-fifth floor—check the floor—I could see Central Park and all the way to the West Seventy-ninth Street Boat Basin. There was a yacht moored in the Hudson River. I started talking the story.

" 'Here's your opening scene. The cameras focus on a yacht tied up off Manhattan. Then we zoom to a bed in a stateroom. It's a big bed. In a big stateroom. The bed has black silk sheets. In the bed, there's a blonde. She's a gorgeous blonde. She's naked—' "

"Stop!" Robbins recalls the executives cried, "We'll buy it!"

"And then what happened?" I asked excitedly. What a relief not to be hearing another one of those dreary Merle Miller tragedies about the Hamlet-like indecisiveness of network executives.

"I went back to France and forgot about it."

At his villa in Le Cannet, Robbins resumed the life of a struggling novelist. He had finished his fourteenth novel, *The Adventurers*, and was having some writing problems with

**165**

the fifteenth, *The Inheritors*. As an escape, he spent the summer working on the screenplay for *The Adventurers*.

"I slaved on that script," he explained. "I worked two hours in the morning and three hours in the afternoon on it for two months." But it all turned to ashes when the film's director didn't like the script. "He said it had too much violence. Too much sex. Too much action. And it was too much like my book." All Robbins got out of that distasteful experience was $250,000.

Was that what made him change his mind about risking his reputation by working for TV?

"No," Robbins said. "What happened was that Paul Gitlin, my lawyer, called me up in France and told me, 'ABC bought your idea.'"

The fifty-three-year-old balding novice TV writer said his first words upon hearing the good news were:

"What idea?"

Gitlin, the lawyer who runs Robbins's creative life, said there was nothing unusual about his client's not having worked out all the details of the plot. "We structure the deal first, and then Harold worries about the writing."

Counselor Gitlin happened to drop by a few minutes after my exclusive interview with Robbins began, I guess because of my fame as an objective reporter. "We can't tell you anything," Gitlin said, "except: 1) Harold wrote a number of books, 2) their titles, 3) they sell very well, 4) they're published in many foreign languages and, 5) Harold has a unique personality, which I don't propose to define."

Gitlin said it was an invasion of privacy to

ask how much money Harold was earning. I knew how he felt; I certainly didn't want to discuss how much *I* was getting for writing about *him*. "Tell him the truth," Harold said. "I can bankrupt three film companies and one broadcasting company next season."

From private sources—Leonard Lyons's column—I learned that the new TV writer's literary contracts alone guarantee him a minimum of $504,000 a year until 1991. So there must have been other factors behind Robbins' decision to make the financial sacrifice and go into TV.

"I want to reach a new audience with television," Robbins explained. "The 30 million nonreaders. A writer, you know, doesn't write for the closet. But it's not as altruistic as it may seem. I may wind up getting only in the low seven figures for this show. If it works, the networks will be able to afford a lousy three or four [million] for my next book."

This is the principle of casting one's bread on the water. But Robbins is doing something even such major writers as Irving Wallace and Jacqueline Susann have never done, for a larger principle: freedom of expression. He objects to the way the movies have censored his books. "While I have the highest respect for Joe Levine, who made *The Carpetbaggers*, he only used 10 percent of the novel. That is a waste of talent. ABC is giving me 100 to 150 hours to tell my whole story, chapter by chapter. Something like that has never been done before."

Actually, the idea of doing a whole novel on television was not as new as ABC, the network of innovation, claimed in its pre-production press releases. The BBC did John Galsworthy's novel *The Forsyte Saga* in a twenty-six-part weekly series. But Robbins would have enough trouble getting his racy view of life through network continuity, I thought, without hearing his concept wasn't original.

"What is the story you have to tell?" I asked, no longer able to contain my curiosity.

"It is that some people survive," the novelist explained, "and others don't survive."

"That sounds like a million bucks," I said in admiration.

"The survivors are the people who set the styles in fashion, morality, everything," Robbins went on, looking out the window of the Plaza, across Central Park to the West Seventy-ninth Street Boat Basin. "It's about the struggle for power within the last of the great banking houses."

The first two shows, he said, had already been shot for $850,000 on location on the Riviera in his neighbor's house, the Rothschild villa. *The Survivors* was going to be another one of those shows about the folks next door.

The last question I asked was whether he would be frustrated as an artist if the network tried to rewrite any of his chapters. "I wouldn't have gone into this if I didn't have complete control of everything," he explained. "I write the same kind of thing whether it's for TV, motion pictures or books. It's my thing."

In the months that followed, I thought of Senator Pastore lying awake nights worrying about the debut of the Harold Robbins show. It had the potential, as a Senator from Rhode Island might phrase it, for unleashing an onslaught of filth on an unsuspecting American public unprecedented in the history of broad-casting.

The reason for Robbins's success as a novel-ist is that he writes about events and acts that people can identify with, what he loosely calls "naturalism." Trying to put Robbins down as a reporter, a critic once asked, "Is an orgy with thirty-eight people real life?"

Robbins answered, "Where have you been, baby?"

I couldn't wait to see what had to be the finest example of hard-core literature ever shown on television. I asked a network man if I could screen the first few chapters of Har-old's work in progress. "Haven't you heard?" he said. "We threw out the shows Harold worked on. We took an $800,000 bath. The stuff didn't work."

In the opinion of the critics at the network, Harold was spending too much time develop-ing motivation of his characters. "He was ex-plaining how a great banking institution really worked. But who cared about banks? The first two episodes were building up, sure, but they were building up to telling us more about banking."

It was the sort of thing one expected to hear if André Malraux or Max Lerner had been paid in the low six figures to develop a story for television.

"We're still using Harold's basic story line and characters," the network man assured me, "but the new writers are adding real plot and subplot. In the middle of the night, Lana gets on the phone and says something like, 'Hire me a jet.' That's what people can identify with. We're emphasizing the controversy over who sired one of the kids in the banking house. And we've written into the story a Greek shipowner who wants to marry Lana."

"You fellows certainly had a lot of nerve adding something like that to Harold's work," I protested.

"Look, if I was you I'd forget all about Harold's role in *The Survivors*," the network man said. "We'll fly you out to the Coast so you can see what *The Survivors* is really like now. It's an all new ball game."

I told the network it might corrupt me. Besides, I'm too busy now organizing a writers committee to protest the suppression of what Harold wanted to say on television. If a man of his stature can't survive the pressures of commercial television, what hope is there for the rest of us? Keep your cards and letters coming to ABC, folks.

---

*Hope for Park Avenue*

On June 20, 1967, an unknown actress made her stage debut in a theater-restaurant in Chicago—unknown in the sense that her name meant nothing in the theater. Few people even knew she had aspirations along these lines, although it was later discovered she had been studying unobtrusively for years with teachers from the Royal Academy of Dramatic Arts in London as well as the London Academy of Music and Dramatics. The Chicago reviews were unanimous.

"She has spunk," wrote drama critic Glenna Syse of the *Sun-Times*.

"She is not yet a stage actress," noted Richard Christiansen of the *Daily News*. "Indeed she may never be one. . . ."

"She has a certain assurance," allowed Ann Marsters of the *American*, "but no style. Her voice has a nice tone, but she does not know how to project it. And what is almost embarrassing to an audience are her inept little gestures. She doesn't know what to do with her hands or arms. . . ."

"A new star is not born," concluded Will Leonard of the *Tribune*.

All of which goes to show how wrong critics can be. On the basis of that initial performance in the comedy *Philadelphia Story* last summer, the American Broadcasting Company courageously decided to give Lee Bouvier the major role in its two-hour special television adaptation of the mystery-drama classic *Laura*. Miss Bouvier plays Laura, an advertising account executive whose face, especially on misty nights, drives men mad.

It took nerve for the network to cast an unknown in such a demanding role when it could have had any one of a number of great actresses for the part—women like Sally Fields, Janice Rule, Wanda Hendrix or Patty Duke. In so doing, the network gave the lie to the current show-biz maxim that to make it big these days you have to be the daughter of somebody famous. (Marlo Thomas, Liza Minnelli, and Nancy Sinatra are often cited to demonstrate this truth.) Lee Bouvier's success proves you can also get ahead today by being the sister of somebody famous.

How did it happen? First, Lee Bouvier had the desire. Being the thirty-four-year-old mother of two; the wife of Prince Stanislas

**171**

Radziwill, an impoverished Polish count who lost everything during World War II and pulled himself up by the bootstraps to become a successful London businessman; one of the beautiful people, who are what is happening— all of these things apparently weren't enough.

A psychiatrist I know best explained the motivation of women with Miss Bouvier's hang-up: When a housewife on Fire Island told him she was returning to college to take her master's in school psychology, he said, "I know, you want to be a *real* person." Miss Bouvier undoubtedly wanted to do something more productive with her life than her sister, who has been reigning as a queen-figure. "I've always loved the theater," Miss Bouvier told a reporter last summer, "and wanted to be part of it." The realization of her dreams gives hope to everybody on Park Avenue.

But none of this explains Lee Bouvier's meteoric rise from the role of Katharine Hepburn in *Philadelphia Story* to Gene Tierney in *Laura*. My guess is that David Susskind, the producer of *Laura*, deserves credit for the idea. His shop isn't known as Talent Associates Ltd. for nothing.

Still other speculation centers around Truman Capote. Miss Bouvier, this school of thought maintains, was merely a pawn in getting Capote to do the adaptation for ABC. He flew to her Chicago opening. "I'm just sort of an old friend," he told interviewers in her dressing room. "She's a hard-working girl doing her level best." When the two flew to Alabama recently to inspect shooting on one of T's projects, Capote's father saw them. "They make a beautiful couple," he observed.

It's a father who knows his own son. The whole relationship is a confusing one. How it all happened really isn't very important anyway, because *Laura* has already been taped.

At the time of her Chicago debut there was a fuss in the press about Miss Bouvier's trying to manage the news. *Women's Wear Daily* charged that its critic had been barred from the opening-night performance. Miss Bouvier denied the trade publication's suggestion that she wanted to avoid a review. To make sure I wouldn't be barred from seeing her debut on TV in some way I haven't quite figured out—could the Kennedys secure an injunction against critics turning on their sets?—I asked ABC to preview the show (a week before it was broadcast in January, 1968). The big news is that this time Lee Bouvier at least equals her last performance.

Capote's adaptation of the Vera Caspary novel, which Otto Preminger turned into a successful and unforgettable movie in 1944 after it failed on Broadway, opens with a shot of Laura in a nightgown. There is a shotgun blast. The next thing we see is Laura stiff as a novice actress lying on a table in a morgue. A fear ran through me. If they were merely trying to exploit Miss Bouvier's name, this might be the end of her performance. Capote is well known for his bizarre sense of humor. More than anything else, I wanted to hear Miss Bouvier's voice, even if it was only in a one-line, roll-on part. Did she sound like Marilyn Monroe, as her sister did?

Several minutes later, Miss Bouvier, who turns out not to be dead at all, speaks her first lines. Arriving at a cocktail party, she says:

"Waldo bought [remainder garbled] . . ." As I mentioned, it was a cocktail party and you couldn't hear anything anybody said, which is true of the dialogue at most cocktail parties. Her next line came in answer to Farley Granger's remark that he knows her because she is famous: "I didn't know I was famous."

It is a beautiful in-joke, which few people will get. Happily, though, Miss Bouvier sounds like a real person. In fact, her characterization is consistently that of a real person. The first major scene, for example, calls for her to stand around at a cocktail party. She looks awkward. It is beautiful acting. That's exactly how everybody stands around at cocktail parties.

Then she dances divinely with Farley Granger. She smiles up at him and runs her hand along the nape of his neck. She does these things naturally. Her naturalness also comes through in the scenes where she combs her hair.

Miss Bouvier does not radiate inner warmth, but her role calls for a cold woman. At times the audience may doubt that such women exist in real life. Anyone who works in an advertising agency, however, knows women account executives are a strange breed.

Unfortunately, Miss Bouvier is still not experienced enough to prevent other performers from stealing her scenes. "Can you cook?" asks Robert Stack, playing the detective who investigates Laura's death. This is where she's really going to have to act, the viewer finds himself thinking. But her devoted maid comes through the kitchen door and throws a fit at seeing the dead woman alive—breaking up the big scene. "Pull yourself together," Miss Bouvier says to the servant, "and make us some breakfast."

The actress's most serious shortcoming in her television debut is her physical appearance. Laura's face is the key to the story: a portrait of Laura hangs over the fireplace in the living room and is responsible for making the detective fall in love with the supposedly dead woman. When Lee Bouvier stands next to her portrait, it is obvious that the portrait painter did not capture her. This may be what is known in the profession as a sight gag. I found it distracting.

"She looks much better in person," explained an ABC spokesman at the screening. Miss Bouvier will go even further in television and movies, I predict, if the cameramen will shoot her out of focus, something they always do for Doris Day.

I am not as sanguine about what Truman Capote is doing to improve the quality of television with his adaptation. That Capote should have been attracted to a gory murder story is not surprising. As George Sanders, the villain who seems to be his spokesman, says twice, "I am fascinated by murders."

Capote has modernized the basic story by making Sanders (in the role made famous in the movie by Clifton Webb) a television commentator instead of a radio commentator. And rock 'n' roll music has replaced the fox trot at the cocktail parties. But Capote's famed ear is off when he has the detective saying he wants to solve the case right away so he can get to an important baseball game between the Orioles and the Yankees. That's right out of the 1950s.

Some people would have liked to see either

**175**

the star or Arlene Francis (who plays the aging seducer of young handsome men less degenerately than Judith Anderson did in the movie) in the nude. Capote has given us, instead, George Sanders.

Where Clifton Webb played his role as a priss, Sanders' homosexuality is blatant. By the final scenes, he is raving about Miss Bouvier's disgusting attraction to he-men like Farley Granger. "Those gross physical types," he screams hysterically. "How could you throw away what we had together on that vulgar little time-server. It was sordid and undignified. . . . You can't rid yourself of your obsessive need for those muscular men. . . . You've soiled Laura's image in the arms of that lousy lout." And so forth.

He also has made crystal clear for the television audience the necrophilia underlying the story. Robert Stack, who played the wholesome Elliot Ness in *The Untouchables*, is shown lying in Laura's bed, drinking scotch and thinking about the dead heroine. There is a knock at the door. "The lady isn't home," Stack says to Sanders. "If I go into the bedroom," responds Sanders with his eyebrows arched, "shall I find your overnight bag? You're liable to wind up on a psychiatric couch if you don't watch out. A detective who has fallen in love with a corpse."

The Capote adaptation of *Laura* will make your blood run cold. It's as if he thought giving us Lee Bouvier was not enough for one night.

At this time of the year it is my custom to give out awards. The TV season has been so mediocre, however, I haven't been able to single out the ten worst shows of 1968. This must come as bad news for the television industry, which lives for recognition.

It may be that I have become jaded over the years; the annals of television criticism are filled with cases of critics who have lost their perspective, as well as their minds. My own theory about why it is difficult to pick the worst shows, though, is that television has been slowly raising its standards. The process is largely imperceptible to the naked eye, but those of us close to the business know something has been going on.

Perhaps it is the influence of the Public Broadcast Laboratory, which week after week since 1967 has been demonstrating the limitations of the medium. Or the emergence in the 1960s of David Susskind as a major source of inspiration at the networks. Or the alarming sophistication of advertising agencies, traditionally a bad influence in the television industry.

Whatever the reason, the bitter truth is that really embarrassing bad shows are as rare today as good shows. (In such a sweeping generalization, of course, I would not include educational television; that is in a class by itself.) One has only to look at the *Dean Martin Show* on NBC to see how depressingly thin the field of terrible shows has grown.

This program was my nominee for the worst show of 1966 and 1967, but I never mentioned it in print before because I was afraid Dean Martin's friends would "get me." A word from

**177**

Frank Sinatra and the editors of this magazine might not have picked up my option, ending a promising career. Now through private sources (a September 1968 issue of *TV Guide*) I have learned that Dino and Frank are drifting apart. "Last fall, when he found it inconvenient to appear at a New York benefit," *TV Guide* reported authoritatively, "he wired Sinatra, 'My ulcer is acting up.'" So I guess it is safe to say what I think of Dean Martin, who last year made television history by signing an unprecedented three-year, no-option NBC contract for $34 million.

I have always had the highest regard for the man personally. There is a streak of honesty in Dino that is unusual in television; for example, when he signed that $34-million contract he said, "God! I am not worth it." Few of us are, even in these days when a dollar doesn't go as far as it once did.

The secret of Martin's success in presenting the worst show of '66 and '67 was his spontaneity. This special effect was not accidental. In fact, it could never have been achieved without Dino's philosophy of not rehearsing.

Other television variety shows are tightly strung together, with everybody seeming to know his place, cues and lines. Indeed, the host and his guests generally appear to have been working together under the careful eye of a merciless director for seventy to eighty hours before the final taping. The ironic result is artificiality. If you can believe Dino, and I do, he spends six days a week at the golf course and drops in on his show just in time to go on the air. In the Golden Age of Dean Martin ('67) the star could always be counted on to accidentally place his hand on some actress's behind or breast—a gesture that always made for an embarrassingly bad program.

The danger of this kind of craftsmanship is that it tends to develop a logic of its own. The production errors come to seem so routinely programmed that they might just as well be inserted by a computer. Predictably, the *Dean Martin Show* has finally lost some of its freshness.

I hate to be the one to say this, but Dino's hour has risen from a classically bad show to a mediocre one. Its new slickness makes it virtually indistinguishable from the other variety shows, with one exception—Dino himself. He remains one of the most offensive $34-million performers in television.

Dino's voice hasn't changed much from 1966 to now. He still sounds like, well, Dean Martin. Frankly, I am not qualified to discuss crooners, given my lack of a musical background. The other thing Dino does on his show is act drunk. Since I've been drinking myself for years, I recognize what a bad actor Dino is.

There has been much discussion in television circles about whether Dean Martin really drinks before he goes on the air. Some people swear they can smell liquor in their living rooms as soon as they turn on NBC Thursday nights. My guess is that Dino is a strict teetotaler.

I don't have any hard facts to support this view, nor am I about to waste my valuable time getting them. According to that reporter at *TV Guide*, it took him "ten months, two weeks and three days" to get into Dino's dressing room to ask a series of probing questions,

**179**

which began with "Tell me, Mr. Martin, is thi
your third or fourth season?" Somehow i
doesn't seem that important to find out Dino'
public position on drinking, especially whe
there is so much circumstantial medical ev
dence that he couldn't possibly be drunk o
television.

To begin with, Dean Martin has an ulcer (o
else he was lying to Frank, and nobody lies t
Frank). True, on his December 26 show Din
so overacted the friendly drunk (squeezin
comedienne Barbara Heller at inappropriat
moments and mumbling his lines with Len
Horne and Buddy Ebsen), that he shook eve
my conviction that this was just a tasteles
performance. But I consulted a leading med
cal authority during the commercial, Dr. Mo
ris Fishbein's *Modern Home Medical Adviser
Illustrated* (along with *The Home Book o
Surgery* it should be in every television den`
Fishbein clearly states that alcohol can have
serious effect on people suffering from ulcers
gastritis, rosacea, gonorrhea, nephrosis an
pregnancy.

It is also hard for me to believe that Dr
David Sarnoff and the stockholders of the Ra
dio Corporation of America would sit idly b
watching a $34-million investment drink him
self to death every Thursday evening—unless
of course, their property was covered by
workman's compensation insurance policy i
excess of that amount. (NBC refused to dis
cuss this with me, claiming it was against the
network's corporate policy.)

Drunks can be charming on television. The
day before Dean Martin went on the air wit
his impersonation of a stoned second-rat

singer, viewers in the New York metropolitan area had the pleasure of watching W. C. Fields belt a few in *The Bank Dick* (WOR). It was Christmas morning, an excellent example of timely programming: it prepared the youngsters for the behavior of adults later in the day. W. C. Fields is required viewing for my children. If they have to drink, I want them to learn how to hold their liquor like a Fields rather than the sloppy Martin.

Lest there be any mistake about the message of *The Bank Dick*, Fields announces several times in the opening scenes that his name is "Sousé—with the *accent grave* on the 'e.'" What a superb well-mannered drinking companion old man Sousé is. Every time he swallows a shot, he takes off his gloves and dips his fingers neatly in the chaser. As a modern education program *The Bank Dick* has only one defect: much of the action takes place in what Fields calls "The Black Pussy Café," and that sort of double entendre, while commonplace on the *Dean Martin Show*, is jarring on a Christmas morning.

Where will the new bad shows come from to replace the void left by the rise of Dean Martin? I saw one earlier last month that seemed to have a lot of potential, an NBC special featuring a new fellow I had never seen on television with the improbable name of Elvis Presley.

The singer wore a leather suit, sweated like a dog under the hot lights, and got down on his knees to sing a song which began, "You ain't nothin' but a hound dog." Then he started twitching uncontrollably as he went into "I'm all shook up/my hands are shaking and my knees are weak." (Dr. Fishbein diagnosed these symptoms as Parkinson's Disease.) Several girls in the studio audience passed out on cue, an overtheatrical touch. The singer's lip curled, and he stopped playing his "big geetar" to pull it down.

"Something wrong with my lip," he said, and the audience went wild. "Don't laugh. I got news for you. This lip got me in twenty-nine movie pictures."

Elvis wiped his face with a handkerchief he grabbed from a girl in the audience. She passed out. I passed out. I told my wife to pass out, too. When we came to ten minutes later, he was lecturing those who had not passed out about the role of gospel music in rock 'n' roll. Then he broke into a temperance lecture which would not be out of place on Dino's show: "I used to smoke and drink/and dance the hootchy (mumble)/Now I'm saved (mumble)/I used to lie and cheat and step on people's feet/Now I'm standing at the door of salvation's (mumble)/I'm saved, Oh yeah."

This man with the odd name and animal magnetism is a born leader, I thought, as I rolled on the floor saving myself. "Goin' do one more song," he said cruelly. "NO, oh God, NO," we groaned all over America.

Then it was over; the geetar man was gone. It was the strangest hour on television last year, and I had the distinct feeling that it was either the worst thing I had ever seen or the best.

The New York outlet of the American Broadcasting Company, WABC-TV, has been winning something of a reputation for a number of locally produced specials—soon to be syndicated nationally—in a field that might be called "popular anthropology." A typical study, titled *The In Crowd*, explored the folkways of a strange breed of people who are said to swing. Through the miracle of modern electronics, TV cameras went right into the natural habitat of these people, an "invitation only" cocktail party in the Penthouse East suite of the New York Hilton Hotel. Thus we were able to observe what they do naturally, which is talk.

We heard the unrehearsed conversation of celebrities, writers, minidressed debs and models. In other words, the just plain beautiful people. Betsy von Furstenberg debated LSD with columnist Max Lerner. Comedian Milt Kamen tried to make out with model Heather Hewett. Michael Dunn explained how things looked from his special vantage point. And Helen Gurley Brown gave viewers some more of her outrageous opinions. Predictably, she turned the conversation to sex. Sometimes I wish Miss Brown would just take a cold shower.

This was an honest show in that the cameras told it to us the way it was. It was quite boring. The fault, though, rests as much with the cocktail party as a communications medium as with the swingers who talked. I'm sure a show based on the conversation of, say, Betsy von Furstenberg and Max Lerner *after* the cocktail party would have stirred broader interest. But this, of course, is not yet possible on televison.

Hopefully we will read about it at some later date in Mr. Lerner's newspaper column.

My appreciation of *The In Crowd* was further handicapped by the fact that I felt uncomfortable being at a party I wasn't really invited to—personally, I mean. Still, the show can be recommended for anyone who has a psychological need to be a member of an "out" group for an hour or less some night.

There is an even wider prospective audience for another of the WABC-TV experimental anthropological studies, titled *Jacqueline Susann and 'Valley of the Dolls.'* It should be required viewing in every creative-writing class.

As you may have heard, Jacqueline Susann is the woman who in her middle years gave up an unpromising career as an actress and glamour girl to write a novel. *Valley of the Dolls*, which exposes the seamier side of the movie business, immediately established her as a muckracking social historian in the tradition of Upton Sinclair, Theodore Dreiser and Rona Jaffe.

Before Miss Susann wrote the book, it was commonplace for agents, studio executives and even critics to take advantage of a girl by telling her they could make her a star. The swine! Today millons of American teenage girls who have read nothing but *Valley of the Dolls* are educated enough to know it is necessary to have talent to achieve lasting success in the movie industry. Sex can help a girl get into a few dozen pictures, and make a few millon dollars, but it all turns to ashes.

Miss Susann also warns our young females that actresses have trouble sleeping at night and must resort to drugs, which can be habit-forming; that they should not sleep in the same bed at finishing schools in Switzerland because an unnatural relationship can spring up; and that handsome men with English accents can have their way with frigid Radcliffe girls. Indeed, there is as much useful information in this one novel as in the combined nonfiction of Helen Gurley Brown.

The ABC televison special, however, did not explore these major discoveries of Jackie Susann's career. Rather, it dealt with her struggles as a woman trying to fulfill herself as a writer. Ever since she was a little girl growing up in Philadelphia, Miss Susann admitted in the special, she had been dreaming of reaching the top. "Mount Everest," she called it.

The theme repeats itself frequently in her published work. "You've got to climb to the top of Mount Everest," are the first words in her novel. They appear, too, on pages 60, 111 and 178 of the Bantam edition of *Valley of the Dolls*—each time echoed by a different character, giving the impression that her people all belonged to the same mountain-climbing club. She explained the metaphor at the end of the TV show by saying, "Mount Everest can be anywhere." One blushes anyway.

When Sir Edmund Hillary describes his early dreams about Mount Everest, it sounds wholesome. In Miss Susann's case, it sounds like a sex dream. But I guess it's better than dreaming about snakes.

At any rate, the special traced Miss Susann's climb to the top, from the Schiffli Embroidery girl on television commercials to the day she arrived in Hollywood and found her name stenciled on the blacktop of the 20th Century–

**185**

Fox parking lot. Eddie Cantor, Miss Susann remembered in one emotional scene, told her never to go to Hollywood "unless they really wanted you. They finally sent for me not as an actress, but as Jacqueline Susann, author."

There were many scenes of what life is really like for an author in Hollywood: The parking lot. Grauman's Chinese Theater. The set of *Peyton Place*. The wardrobe room during the making of *Valley of the Dolls*. These sequences, which may make some people think the whole special was nothing but a cheap publicity gimmick for plugging her movie, proved once again that underneath the tinsel of Hollywood there is tinsel. I'm surprised that Miss Susann went along with this kind of exploitation of her real talent as a writer.

I don't think the producers of this special really understood their subject. They treated Miss Susann as if she were a publishing phenomenon, the one-book author. But she isn't a George Plimpton fooling around in publishing. No less an authority on the subject than Irving Mansfield, her husband, says she is a serious writer, already hard at work on her second novel.

The producers found it necessary to interview a number of other writers, most of them members of her literary set, on Miss Susann's qualifications as a novelist. Noel Bohn, author of *The Kremlin Letters*, unhesitatingly declared, "She's damned good." Victor Lasky observed, "A lot of dirty books aren't making the grade like Jackie's." Helen Gurley Brown and Rona Jaffe also appeared in cameo roles. Miss Jaffe gushed, "I think her success is a real groovy thing." That's really the way Miss Jaffe writes. Miss Susann is no Flaubert stylistically, but who is these days? She's certainly as good a writer as Rona Jaffe.

What made this special a document of lasting significance to belles-lettres was the advice Miss Susann gave about the craft of writing a best seller. I pass along her instructions for what they are worth.

Miss Susann uses a typewriter. Goodman Ace gave the author her first typewriter, a portable. It was this gift that really started her writing career: "You know what I told him the other day? I said, 'Just think, Goody, what might have happened if you'd given me a piano —by now I'd be in Carnegie Hall.'" Currently she is using a standard office typewriter.

She works seven or eight hours a day, she reassured the TV audience. "You just have to force yourself to go to the typewriter. It's like giving up cigarettes." She writes five drafts of a novel. The first is on "inexpensive white paper." She doesn't try to develop characters until the second draft, which is on yellow paper. The third draft is on pink. The fourth on blue. The final draft is on good white paper. Miss Susann explained that she never varies from this ritual. One doesn't argue with success.

To keep track of her characters, she uses a large blackboard in her writing den, or "torture chamber." The characters are color-coded. Each character's name is in a different-colored chalk so that she knows at a glance in which draft a character first appears.

Miss Susann believes it's the novelist's job to write about the things she knows. "Ever since writing began," she explained, "writers start with a germ of an idea. Somewhere, something he's seen." That's the technique she follows.

"Many people say the character of Ann in *Valley of the Dolls*," she revealed, "is based on Grace Kelly. Well, we're both from Philadelphia. When I wrote about Ann I wanted to write about Everygirl. There's a Jennifer at every country club. I saw a picture of Jayne Mansfield and got the idea of giving Jennifer extra-large breasts."

After a hard day at the typewriter, Miss Susann knocks off work and goes to a gym. This is important because she finds writing "enlarges the waist of the writer."

I would have liked Miss Susann to go a little deeper into the meaning of writing—for example, to tell us the best way to handle capital gains, depletion of natural resources, and writing off vacation travel expenses as research. But the program was produced for a general audience.

Despite all her instructions on writing, which on the whole I found quite sound, Miss Susann ended the special by crediting her success to her husband, Irving. "I can accomplish anything," she proclaimed, "as long as Irving Mansfield is my husband. Without him I couldn't be a whole person." Obviously every young struggling novelist should get a muse named Irving.

The relationship of the author and her husband, who has devoted his life since 1966 to pushing his wife's book, sounds like one of the great love stories of all time. I'm sure the television industry executive who claims she heard

Irving say recently, "The way Jackie is carrying on, you'd think she wrote that book," heard wrong.

---

# THE GREAT
# INSTITUTIONS

---

For some reason the major networks didn't give the recent hearings held by the Senate Subcommittee on Communications the full coverage they deserved. The minute or two they received on the evening news shows served to satisfy only the integrity of the various news departments. National Educational Television rushed into the information vacuum the very night of the hearings with an hour-long special featuring the testimony of the big network presidents on the role of violence in commercial broadcasting, but unfortunately the show was biased. At least I have never seen network presidents looking so bad on TV.

The subcommittee chairman, Senator John O. Pastore (D.-R.I.), gave me the impression he had been over this ground before—that this was another installment in a kind of soap opera, called *As the Worm Turns*. His script, which sounded well researched, bordered on contempt.

For continuity, Pastore opened the soap opera by saying, in effect, that there is too much violence on television. What, he demanded to know, are the networks going to do about it?

*Of Presidents and Panelists*

189

Dr. Frank Stanton, president of CBS, gave his customary persuasive performance with his traditional aria, *"Mea Culpa."* He denied there is too much violence on the tube, and insisted that what there is of it is necessary for plot development. Art, Stanton implied, follows life.

Even if there is too much violence, the good doctor-president pointed out, the broadcasters have their own internal police force, the widely feared National Association of Broadcasters. Nothing on *The Smothers Brothers* show last season (1969) matched the Pastore-Stanton exchange that followed on why CBS didn't permit the dreaded NAB censors to see his network's violent shows *before* they went on the air.

Stanton was supported by a star-studded cast of two: Julian Goodman, president of NBC-TV, and Elton Rule, head of ABC-TV. NBC's performance, it seemed to me, did not measure up to the standard set by CBS. I blame that on inexperience: this was only Goodman's second appearance before the panel. His eager-to-please, deferential tone was enhanced by a soft Kentucky accent. Margarine could have melted in Goodman's mouth as he came out in favor of less violence on television. He said he had a six-year-old child at home, and knew from personal experience why better shows were needed.

Rule, who was making his debut before the subcommittee, shows promise. The handsomest of the three presidents (this is one area where ABC is ahead of the other networks), he resembled Sonny Tufts both in looks and in his gift of gab as he handled the senators' questions. Rule provided the touch of comic relief needed to make the hearings work as entertainment as well as education.

In all fairness, the subcommittee members were playing fast and loose with Rule when they trapped him into a discussion of the program *Turn On*. One good thing you could say about that limp "Son of *Laugh-In*" is that it was nonviolent. It may have been smutty, but this wasn't a hearing on the role of soft-core pornography on TV.

The senators appeared to be trying to gain an insight into the broadcasting decision-making process in pressing Rule for an explanation of what turned him off on his new show after only one performance. Rule seemed just as puzzled by the sudden turn of events as the rest of us. He would have been wiser to take the Fifth Amendment than to encourage the Senate to get into an area where it has no special expertise. A president with a quicker mind could have easily turned the conversation around to a discussion of senatorial decisions.

The hearings proved there is more diversity in network presidents than in network programs. Still, if I were a television stockholder (which I am not, because of the obvious conflict of interest), I would have been very upset with top management's performance at the Pastore hearings. These network presidents, I have heard, are ruthless men. Yet they came to Washington with hats in their hands and feet in their mouths. If humility is supposed to be the strategy, the stockholders' interests would be better served by character actors, who could put on a more facile performance.

No matter how much the presidents may try

to appear unaware of program content, they will have a hard time convincing anybody there isn't too much violence. The senators are not stupid. Obviously, the networks have a vested interest in violence—good, solid, economic reasons for wanting to maintain the status quo in the ratio of violent to nonviolent programming. Senators can understand the pocketbook approach. The public wants violence, and a network can't say the public be damned any more than a senator can every six years.

Stockholders have the right to expect their top executives to stand behind their programming decisions. My advice to Stanton, Goodman and Rule, all of whom will be back soon for another thrilling installment, is to exercise leadership and come out firmly for violence. It is an issue worth fighting for to the death.

As much as the network brass, incidentally, I was alarmed by the new pugnacity of the subcommittee. These senators seem to fancy themselves critics. Now while it may be true that, unlike the other arts, everybody who watches television is a critic, some members of the Subcommittee on Communications appear to have only a passing knowledge of the field. Senator Pastore, of course, is a man of stature who could easily replace Jack Gould at *The New York Times*. But I was dismayed by Senator Daniel Inouye (D.-Hawaii). His major contribution was to hold up a newspaper ad for a TV showing of *La Dolce Vita* and ask how long this has been going on. Senator Philip Hart (D.-Mich.) may be a John Wayne on consumer problems, but he is a Wally Cox on television. And Senator Frank Moss (D.-Utah) asked questions that sounded as if he were sitting at the wrong hearing. My conclusion is that it would not be in the public interest for the Senate to run the networks.

As long as I am in a critical mood, I would like to say a bad word about one of the panelists on a recent episode of *Critique*, Stanley Kauffmann's generally brilliant and entertaining review of the arts. The subject was the movie *Greetings*, an aboveground sex-draft-Vietnam protest currently playing in New York. The senator from Hawaii would have enjoyed the scenes from *Greetings* which the *New Republic* critic used to introduce his subject, even though the best, or dirtiest, parts were cut.

Kauffmann then interviewed the two young important film makers, whose names I have forgotten, on their craft. "We don't get hung up on the words, those hundred-page scripts," one of them said, explaining his contribution to the cinematic art. "If the actors memorize their lines with us, they're dead." The other innovator added, "If you try to remember what you said before, you go stale."

After the technical aspects of the work of art are explained on *Critique*, Kauffmann holds a broader discussion with his panelists about what it all means. Critic Margot Hentoff said she didn't experience any kind of shock at what these revolutionaries had presented on the screen. A beautiful woman in a pants suit, she came over very well cinematographically, although she did sound a lot like that other critic with her same last name, something bound to happen to anybody living with Nat Hentoff.

**193**

The discussion took a turn for the worst with the next panelist, Marvin Kitman. When moderator Kauffmann asked how he felt about the film, he explained that he had a gut reaction to New Wave films. Hand-held cameras gave him motion sickness. "As a matter of fact," Kitman continued, "before I came to the studio to discuss this picture, I had to take a Dramamine."

The panelist said that because he was not an authority on films, he assumed that Kauffmann had invited him as an expert on military affairs. Pointing out that he was a veteran, he declared: "I am against the draft, and think it should be ended after everybody has served his time."

Since I was familiar with the panelist's remarks, what Kitman said was not nearly so interesting to me as the interplay between him and the moderator. "Let me pursue what you just said," Kauffmann would continually interrupt. Another time: "Perhaps I can carry on your thought this way. . . ." And: "Which leads to something else. . . ." Or: "I don't want to put words in your mouth. . . ." At first the panelist always looked relieved at having the famed critic carry the ball for a rhetorical touchdown. But then he looked puzzled when the star ran in another direction.

I thought this was only a coincidence until a friend of mine pointed out that this is an integral part of TV debating, which he calls the "You Steal My Thunder and I'll Steal Yours Syndrome." Two people are debating on TV, he explained. One of them finishes his statement by gratuitously wrapping up his opponent's argument, inaccurately, and then asking if that, in fact, is a valid summary of his position. In the history of television discussion shows, there has not yet been anyone who has said, "No, that's not what I'm saying at all." According to my informant, the ploy works something like this:

SEVAREID: So, Mister Nixon, what you seem to be saying is that the late General Eisenhower was a do-nothing President who lulled the country into a false sense of security, right?

NIXON: Right! Right! Eisenhower was a vigorous President who helped forge the dynamic foreign policy we needed.

I learned a lot from my first appearance on a panel show. For one thing, if you're going to be ironic, you'd better wink at the moderator. The network presidents might try this technique the next time they are summoned by the Pastore subcommittee.

---

*Gift of Gab*

Since the medium is the message, I did not feel guilty during the President's State of the Union speech (1968) about concentrating on his TV style rather than his arguments. Surely, no politician has ever projected his personality more effectively on television than President Lyndon Baines Johnson.

He makes a much better impression than any of his predecessors. He has the gift of gab, compared to Calvin Coolidge. He is more photogenic than William Howard Taft. And his speech is more pleasing to the ear than was the squeaky adenoidal voice of Abraham Lincoln. He also sounds a lot less like the politician than Lincoln did. Today we often forget that President Lincoln was the candidate of the *Chicago Tribune* and was even more popular with the business interests than President Johnson is. While Lincoln was making a name for himself in the civil-rights field, his administration was quietly giving away much of the nation's natural resources to the railroad barons.

Set in their ways, politicians have never fully understood the potential of the television medium. In the beginning, they used it as though it were radio. Men stood in front of microphones and delivered speeches as sonorously as possible, hoping the pancake make-up would conceal their double chins. I remember reading a John Crosby column in the old *New York Herald Tribune* which named Thomas E. Dewey as the first office seeker to stumble upon the proper way to use television.

"Dewey threw away the script," Crosby wrote at the time of the New York gubernatorial election in 1950. "He answered questions, as it were, from the floor—the floor being a dozen street corners all over the state of New York. He spoke extemporaneously; he moved from spot to spot, picking up state reports and documents; he sat on the edge of his desk; he scratched his head. . . ." What television did for Dewey was humanize him. It gave the people a chance to see what he was really like—which may be the reason for his subsequent decline in politics.

President Kennedy used television in a limited way. He showed the people only his good side. In contrast, Johnson will go down in history as the first politician to use television to show us all his sides. You can't expect any more from the medium than that.

"When you talk to him in person," explained a former resident of the White House with whom I discussed the President's TV presence, "he's a likable person. When he walks out of the room and goes on camera something happens to him. He becomes a sanctimonious, pious prig."

That's the good side of him.

All men have mean streaks, which usually only their wives get to see. But Lyndon Johnson shows his right on television. No credibility gap here. An unforgettable example of this facet of his personality came through in a program entitled *A Conversation with the President*.

The show started out like a fireside chat, with President Johnson playing the role of FDR, minus the cigarette holder. As he explained his homilies for solving the cities' problems, Frank Reynolds, the clean-cut ABC White House correspondent, interrupted. "Mr. President. In the ghettos I think they'd say that's just talk. White man's talk. What's your reaction to that?"

The President wheeled slowly in his rocking chair and gave Reynolds the coldest stare in the history of television journalism. Undaunted, Reynolds pressed Johnson on what he was really going to do. The President then asked in reply: "What would *you* do, Frank?"

Had the President asked that question of Walter Lippmann or James Reston, he would have gotten recitations from their latest columns; and the country would have been better off. Lacking the proper background, Reynolds would have been wise merely to quote the words of President Eisenhower, who first said, "Well, I wouldn't know about that." Or even, "I'll have a statement on that later." Instead, he weakly insisted the television audience was more interesting in hearing not Reynolds' proposals but the President's.

Having skewered the reporter, the President gave him two or three turns, which every journalist in America felt. "What is your answer, though?" he persevered, as Reynolds hemmed and hawed. "What's your solution, Frank? . . . You're not going to answer now; you're not going to give us your recommendations, your thoughts?"

Finally Reynolds gave his program, which turned out to be a collection of Great Society platitudes. "That's what we're doing," the President triumphed. "And we accept your recommendations, and we are going to carry them out."

Frank Reynolds will never be the same. But I have a feeling that the majority of the non-working press in the country liked the way Lyndon Johnson handled the press. Everybody knows the President has bad manners, and it's a comfort to see them displayed so gracefully on television. One need only imagine Richard Nixon under the pressures of a stress interview to appreciate the grandeur of President Johnson's style in the medium.

And after seeing the master several times on TV in recent months, I found watching the Republicans in their rebuttal to his State of the Union message like watching a college debating team in action. This is not to say the

Republicans have not learned from past mistakes in the medium. Their make-up men, for example, did a masterful job on the debaters who appeared on *The State of the Union: A Republican View* (CBS). There wasn't a trace of five-o'clock shadow on Representative May of Washington as she lashed out at the Johnson Administration's failure to hold the line on consumer prices.

The Congresswoman was only one of seventeen flawlessly made up Republican leaders who went before the people on this major political broadcast—major because it revealed a significant shift in Republican strategy. Instead of discussing mere issues, the Republicans this year will be running on their personalities.

With the titular leader of the show-biz wing of the party, Senator George Murphy of California, as host, the Republicans ran the debate like a variety show. Rather than rely on the grand old men of the party to answer LBJ, Murphy tried out a number of untested new acts. The party seemed to be taking the pulse of the nation to see which type will make the biggest hit in this fall's elections.

First came the young type, Representative William A. Steiger of Wisconsin, famous in the House for being only twenty-nine years old. "No beatnik he," Murphy noted, introducing the rather colorless man who struck me as a young fogey.

Next they needed a photogenic type, which led to the TV debut as a political leader of Representative Robert Mathias of California. Political observers agree that Bob Mathias is probably the best athlete in Congress. The most frequently asked question in the last Congressional session, according to usually reliable informed sources, was "Which one is Bob Mathias?" The boys in the House Press Gallery told visitors, "Just look for the one with the muscles and the comb."

The former Olympic track star had obviously been directed to hide his comb during his four-minute turn on camera. "You know I have faced some high hurdles in my day," he said in a vague opening allusion to his past. Then Representative Mathias leaped to the defense of the poor American farmer, proving he will be a double threat.

Representative Charlotte Reid "from the great state of Illinois" was on the show as a mother type. She warned, "We must be certain the rifles our sons carry in battle do not jam." And possibly because Murphy felt we needed to hear somebody named Poff, he gave us next Representative Richard Poff "of the great state of Virginia." In an accent that made LBJ sound like a damn Yankee, Representative Poff, a symbol of the emerging Republican South, went on to proclaim, "Rape is commonplace in our streets." That sounded like old-fashioned campaign oratory.

The real hit of *George's Show*, however, was Representative Gerald Ford. Taking President Johnson's metaphor about the "great ship of state," Ford sailed it right out of the old ball park. Ford's oratory deserves to be memorized by every American schoolboy. Most children probably missed it because the program didn't go on the air until past their bedtime, so I am taking the liberty of jotting down his concluding paragraphs:

His ship of state is wallowing in a storm-tossed sea, drifting towards the rocks of domestic disaster, beaten by the waves of a world-wide fiscal crisis. The captain should return to the bridge.

We need a captain who will seize the helm, call up full power, break out new charts, hold our course steadfast, and bring us through the storm.

We need a captain who inspires his crew to heroic endeavor. We need a captain with courage to clear the deck and jettison the deadweights; a captain who learned his seamanship beyond the Potomac.

It's no time to abandon ship. It's time for all hands to man their action stations. Let's not give up the ship. America has weathered many terrible storms, rescued many a weaker vessel. It will do it again.

Representative Ford was sent below decks after mopping up the Democrats, but was called back by host Murphy to give viewers "a thirty-second wrap-up on the Republican party's position." Unfortunately, CBS cut him off in mid-sentence to make way for its next program. That left us at sea without a paddle, so to speak.

---

These notes on television's coverage of the Republican National Convention are being transcribed at a time when the nation is gathering strength to watch the Democrats. It's hard to see how the two major networks will be able to make the Chicago proceedings seem more exciting than the Miami convention. But I'm sure they'll manage.

The networks have a need to perform this public service twice within one month every four years. They are like the hero who saves

*The Way It Wasn't*

**201**

somebody from drowning after pushing the poor person into the water. The dramas they report are often the same ones they've created.

There really has not been an open convention in national politics since 1924. That was the year the Democratic Party took 103 ballots to pick John William Davis of West Virginia. He was the best of the sixty candidates whose names were placed in nomination and seconded at great length.

As usual, NBC and CBS worked hard this year to give the impression there was a statistical chance the GOP convention wasn't locked up. In five days and nights of expert analysis, they made it clear the Republican presidential nomination would go to Richard Nixon, Nelson Rockefeller or Ronald Reagan. Lightning could strike anytime between the first ballot, as the Nixon camp suggested, and the ninth or tenth ballot, as Harold Stassen said. The vice presidential nomination, on the other hand, would go to any of the dozens who had been promised second place on the ticket. The polls had been saying substantially the same thing all year.

Actually, Rockefeller and Reagan were battling each other for the divorce vote, which is quite large when you throw in all those who are unhappily married. As all the signs plainly said, Nixon was the one. "Nixon enjoys charisma," ABC newsman Howard K. Smith observed early in the race. On the charismatic scale, Nixon's reading is minus. His real strength in the Republican Party is that he has the image of a winner. Nixon hasn't lost an election since 1962. It was all over, as far as I was concerned, when the prominent New

202

Yorker revealed at a press conference that he was soft on communism. This made him more likable to the liberal traitors he always claimed were selling out the country to Russia.

A cynic might think that the wait-and-see posture taken by NBC and CBS was motivated by the $15-million investment they had in their coverage. Without a race, Gulf Oil and B. F. Goodrich might conclude the democratic processes are no longer viable, and decide there's nothing in the American political system for them in 1972.

With its eyes more openly on the rating charts, ABC decided what the Republican National Convention was worth as a news event. They gave it ninety minutes a night. There was jubilation at ABC corporate headquarters when a rerun of *Garrison's Gorillas* walloped Nixon's regulars by five Arbitron points. It's understandable why this happened. That show is going off the air next season, while the candidates will be around all fall.

ABC has always been third in the hearts of the nation's voters, and I don't think it will lose any ground as a result of its unconventional coverage. The problem with watching ABC during the conventions, however, is that you always have the vague feeling you're missing something.

Anybody who watched ABC the night of the balloting, for example, couldn't get caught up in the Walter Hickel for President movement because the minor network didn't show it. Good old Wally, as Representative Pollock of Alaska explained in his nominating speech, is the Horatio Alger figure who came to Alaska with a borrowed five-dollar bill in his pocket and rose through the rank and file to become governor. At the point where a boomlet was developing for Wally in American homes, he rushed to the podium to deny that he was a candidate.

The ABC viewers also missed seeing delegate Clark McGregor of Minnesota check for his wallet after talking to NBC reporter John Chancellor about the machinations for the vice presidency at the convention. ABC's newsmen were exceptionally waspish, though, in their abridged version. "The delegates seem to be just sitting there," Frank Reynolds said about a report of delegate movement from one camp or another, "enjoying the convention, if enjoying is the proper word." He referred to Governor Reagan as "Ronnie, baby." Of another governor's possible appeal on the ticket in the vice presidential slot, Reynolds said, "Oh yes, Romney does very well in the cities, like Detroit."

A promising addition to the jaded television press corps—David Brinkley seemed especially sour this year—the inexperienced Reynolds will have to learn it is impossible to make a mockery of a convention. The professional politicians already do this too well. Very Special Correspondent Art Buchwald ran into the same problem covering his first convention for CBS.

The use of ridicule at ABC may have been caused by the frustration that network's reporters felt at not being able to ask as many dumb questions as the other networks' men. The best example of this genre so far was Mike Wallace's interview with Julie Nixon. "Do you get a little jealous of your sister?" asked the

CBS newsman about the attention being paid by the press to her younger sibling rival, Tricia. Miss Nixon didn't respond: "Yes, as I was telling my psychiatrist just this morning. . . ."

Still, TV's full color coverage of the GOP meeting did have its bright spots. You saw nice movies about Miami Beach. There was the Fontainebleau in all its Flatbush Moderne beauty; the fabled Moulin Rouge motel with its marquee reminding the home viewer, "Have Your Next Affair Here"; and the Grant Wood-like Georgia delegation marching into caucus in a suite named the Ivory Tower.

The anchor men were veritable fountains of knowledge. Walter Cronkite, my favorite source of trivia, explained during one lull in the proceedings that the balloons, which played a pivotal role in the organized spontaneous demonstrations, cost a penny a piece. He added that the unions charge the candidates thirty-three cents each to fill them up, presumably with hot air. "The Reagan people," CBS viewers learned, "are upset with the position of their balloons in the nets over the rear end of the hall. But they said they can live with it."

The most regrettable thing about the major networks' adherence to their contrived dramas of the past was that this prevented them from sharing one of the biggest news stories in modern political history with the audience: Nixon was telling the truth. The convention followed precisely the scenario he had written.

Rocky used to look like a million on television. He had the image of a man who was warmly squeezing your arm when he talked.

But I fear that the uncritical reporting of exchanges like this one with NBC's Ray Scherer gives him Nixon's old mantle:

Q. Have you caught up to Nixon?

A. Yes, I really have.

Q. What is your strategy?

A. I can tell you this. Nixon has 550 votes. I'll start off with about 280. On the second ballot, there'll be erosion in Nixon's strength. The erosion will continue in the third ballot. I should get it by the fourth.

Q. Why will the delegates go to you, not Reagan?

A. [My notes read: Exceptionally long pause here.] I can win. . . . As Lincoln said, 'Before you can become a statesman, you have to get elected.'

"The erosion went the wrong way," he explained in a conference with reporters after the votes had been counted. Then he thanked the press vigorously and individually. Thank you, Eddie; thank you, George; thank you, Joe; and so forth. Obviously this wasn't Rocky's last press conference.

Coverage of Republican conventions has undoubtedly improved since 1860. Then a man standing on the roof of the convention hall in Chicago, the Wigwam, yelled down the results to the party workers in the streets. Seward led on the first ballot, and his supporters went wild. That was a very important election in the history of the Republican party, as ABC's Sam Donaldson observed in a one-minute essay on the improvement of communications at conventions. If Lincoln hadn't come from behind on the third ballot, the GOP would be known today as the party of Seward.

What the people in the streets didn't know was that Lincoln's managers swung the proceedings around by promising Cabinet posts to delegates right on the convention floor. Television has driven the hard business of the convention off the floor.

The real drama at a convention now goes on in closed rooms. This is where responsible journalists should be in one way or another in this electronic age. The delegate who taped Nixon's remarks on open housing had a better story than the CBS newsman who asked delegate Clark Reed of Mississippi outside a caucus room, "What happened inside?"

"My prediction is Nixon," he said of the talks with Nixon's masterminds, "but it could go either way."

---

## Mr. and Miss Illinois

Forty-nine candidates were defeated in the Miss America race at Convention Hall in Atlantic City this year (1968) for reasons that were never made clear to the television audience. Not that it mattered which candidate emerged triumphant from the final roll call. Men of good will always tend to forget their differences after the convention is over, and get behind the winner. Whatever we may think of Miss Illinois as a woman, I'm sure we will all support her in 1969. As I said of Debra Dene Barnes, who wasn't my first choice for Miss America of 1968, "I can live with her."

Nevertheless I wish NBC would stop covering an event of such importance to womankind so superficially. In the two hours the network devoted to the Pageant, one could hardly distinguish between the personalities of the fifty states' standard bearers, much less discover what, if anything, they stood for.

The spectacle was even more frustrating than usual this year because I gave it my undivided attention. Coming on the heels of another convention, which all the experts were saying had wide impact, I was rather hoping that Miss Wisconsin or Miss New Hampshire would throw Convention Hall into an uproar by shouting that the winner was nothing but a dirty old whore.

NBC didn't join this convention until its final two hours. The candidates, led by Miss Alabama, walked across the stage, bringing everybody up to date on the developments missed the first two nights.

The Queen Mother, Miss Barnes, looked happier than the last time I saw her in 1967—by the end of the night, she would finally be able to wipe that smile off her face. The permanent chairman, Bert Parks, still looked like that happy-go-lucky fellow who was the trademark at George C. Tilyou's Steeplechase. And Bess Myerson once again was in the anchor booth high above the convention floor, raising the religious issue. Miss America of 1945 can do this by her mere presence at these WASP-dominated beauty contests. This year, however, I felt she appeared a bit more militant than usual, wearing on her bosom a diamond-studded six-pointed star.

By great coincidence, the states failed to send any black beauties to the national convention. I don't mean to imply that the minorities were completely without representation.

Miss Alaska may have been of Eskimo ancestry, although she didn't look it.

None of the candidates lost because of their figures or faces, which without exception were above average. And it was not because of their clothes; these looked like they were right off the racks at J. C. Penney. I have been advised that no secretary today would dare wear Miss America's clothes, unless she was trying to be camp. The hems of the late-1950s styles had been raised an inch or two.

The most qualified candidates for the job are usually discovered during the so-called talent competition. Ten semifinalists receive about three minutes each to do their thing. I hoped one of the candidates would recognize the changes that have taken place in the cinema and theater since last year by appearing on stage naked. But mostly they just sang and danced. Miss New York, however, shattered one of the Convention Hall's oldest traditions by displaying real talent as an opera singer. She didn't get past the semifinals, thus saving us from a credentials fight.

Of the five finalists, at least two of the front runners seemed to offer a real choice. Miss Illinois stood for brawn and Miss Massachusetts for brains.

Judith Anne Ford, better known as Miss Illinois, is an eighteen-year-old college physical-education major. She did a number of tricks on the trampoline to demonstrate her physical fitness. Doing a split or waiting for the orchestra to give her a drum roll before flying through the air, Miss Illinois was unflappable. Even upside down, her blond bouffant hairdo did not get mussed. My adviser explained it probably was set in cement. One thing can be said for Miss Illinois's act: It proved conclusively that she was fit.

Miss Massachusetts sang a song in the sign language of the deaf and dumb, an effective way to reach her audience. A speech therapy major at college, Miss Massachusetts spoke exceptionally well with her hands. Actually television hadn't seen anything like it since Mayor Joseph L. Alioto of San Francisco put Vice President Humphrey's name in nomination at Chicago.

Like the other candidates, Miss Massachusetts won all the primaries in her state before Atlantic City. Still, she found time to work with the physically handicapped during summer vacations, as she explained in the traditional last-minute appeal to the judges. Despite her compassion, sensitivity, intelligence and resemblance to Ava Gardner, Miss Massachusetts finished second to Miss Illinois. John Chancellor and Sandor Vanocur weren't on the floor to explain how this could have happened. My theory is that Miss Massachusetts had the misfortune of being behind the times, possibly by as much as ten days.

Nobody could argue that Miss Illinois was the most talented or most beautiful woman at Atlantic City. The country, as represented by the Miss America judges, a cross-section ranging from Ed McMahon to soprano Licia Albanese, was in the mood for a show of strength. We wanted our Miss America to be strong, decisive and unflappable, a leader who wouldn't fall on her head under pressure. A poll of the judges might indicate otherwise, but it's possible that Miss Illinois won for no better reason than that the judges sought to demonstrate their support for what went on at the other convention we've had on television within the last few weeks.

The most beautiful and talented did not win at the Chicago International Amphitheatre either. Mr. Illinois, better known as Mayor Daley, didn't even quite match the high standards set by Miss Illinois for unflappability. True, no matter what went wrong at his beauty contest, his hair never came undone as he sat on his throne in the Illinois delegation. But he reddened when Mr. Connecticut (Senator Ribicoff) gave him credit for inspiring the events ouside, and lost his temper once or twice. Underneath his chiseled Irish marble exterior, Mr. Illinois was human.

While I'm handing out laurels, I'd like to praise Mr. California for solving one of television's major problems in covering politics. Jesse (Big Daddy) Unruh has long been known as the thinking man's political boss, so it should not be surprising that he figured out the way to circumvent Section 315 of the FCC code, the equal-time statute barring national TV debates. Unruh simply invited Messrs. Minnesota and South Dakota to a little gathering with his people which happened to be covered by television cameras.

I'm not sure the two major candidates want to hear any further discussion about national TV debates. Each has been following a strategy of invisibility in the 1968 campaign. Nixon isn't planning to visit every state in the Union this year. Humphrey is planning to break off campaigning every fourth day or so and retire to his ranch house in Waverly, Minnesota. There hasn't been such an unorthodox tactic since Henry Cabot Lodge took afternoon naps in 1960.

The public wants the confrontations, though, and they are worth the political risks. Actually debating can only hurt the front runner. Since professional politicians at the conventions considered both men losers, neither has reason to fear a debate.

Neighbors gather at my house in Leonia, New Jersey, for political *kaffeeklatsches* from time to time, and we'd be honored to have the candidates drop by to test Jesse Unruh's theory. As I wrote to Norman Sheridan and Herbert Klein, the Humphrey and Nixon press secretaries, "If you can fit this into your candidate's schedule, I'm sure the networks will be able to cover it."

On the chance that Sheridan and Klein think I'm only kidding around, I'd like to assure them that my ranch-style house has new wiring, and the members of the discussion group have already worked out the ground rules for the debate. Robert Glatzer's Rules of Order will govern the evening. These include:

1. Credentials will be checked at the front door.

2. Wipe feet on the mat in the entrance hall.

3. Only two drinks before dinner.

4. Don't bring up Vietnam at dinner.

Over the coffee and cigars, each candidate will be asked to address himself to a number of philosophical questions, such as whether a man in politics has the right to change his mind. Then specific questions on the issues will be directed at each man.

To Mr. Nixon: "Will you use the same talent scouts you used to find Spiro Agnew in putting together your cabinet?"

To Vice President Humphrey: "Marvin Garson is in jail in Chicago. Some kids were accused of having stoned a car. The police allege that Garson had a rock in his hand. Will you be putting in a telephone call to Barbara Garson, as President Kennedy called Mrs. Martin Luther King Jr. during the last television debates?"

To Mr. Nixon: "Obscenity appears to be a major Republican issue in 1968. You used the word 'shaft' on TV in your last campaign. *The Dictionary of American Slang* defines that verb as, '2. Having someone insert something, as a barbed shaft, up one's rectum.' Are you against smut when others use it, or is it acceptable when politic?"

To Vice President Humphrey: "You have questioned the propriety of people coming to Chicago during a political convention to demonstrate. Do you feel groups such as the Wisconsin delegation had the right to come to Chicago?"

And so forth, until the moderator says, "Thank you, Mr. Presidential Candidates."

Some people may think these questions have nothing to do with those matters which will concern the President in the next four years. But it is important to remember the big issue in the 1960 TV debates was Quemoy and Matsu.

*Who's Who in the Nixon Administration*

I want to make one thing perfectly clear. My purpose in writing this article is to disavow any responsibility for the advice the President has received on appointments so far. More specifically, I had nothing to do with the bad appointments.

I first heard that I was being drafted as a presidential adviser through *The New York Times*. The story last December said the Nixon talent hunters were soliciting all 64,988 *Who's Who in America* listees for their recommendations on how to fill two thousand top jobs.

Privately, it seemed to me a hell of a way to run a government. I always thought a new administration was supposed to give out jobs to its friends and supporters. Besides, when I was elected to *Who's Who*'s Class of 1968–69 (Volume 35), I assumed that my only responsibility was to serve as a source of inspiration to the nation's youth and bibliophiles.

Then the Nixon administration placed this additional burden on us. As a Republican who believes deeply in the free-enterprise system, I can say candidly that the *Who's Who* plan offended my principles. In the campaign, candidate Nixon had often said that the federal government should aid the private-enterprise sector of the economy. Therefore, if Mr. Nixon didn't have enough friends to fill all the good jobs, why didn't his recruitment team turn to the executive talent agencies on Madison Avenue? The only excuse I could think of was that the economizers in the Nixon inner circle, after losing their hard fight against a higher presidential salary, wanted to save money on the agency fees.

But I decided to help out anyway. Richard Nixon has always been something of a political hero to me. The secret of his success is that he didn't know when he wasn't wanted. He never gave up. The American people finally elected him because he had no place else to go. This kind of success story has appeal to former Republican presidential candidates like Harold Stassen and myself.

What the Nixon people were doing by publicizing their *Who's Who* program was spreading the credit around in advance for the caliber of their appointments. This is known as credit by association. After the talent hunters discovered Spiro T. Agnew last summer, I felt it was in my own best interest to help the President get the right men. I would have preferred a larger role in public life, but the phone never rang. We also serve who only stand and advise.

"As you may know," said Mr. Nixon's letter to the *Who's Who* listees, as quoted in *The New York Times*, "I have pledged to bring into this administration men and women who by their qualities of youthfulness, judgment, intelligence and creativity can make significant contributions to our country. I seek the best minds in America to meet the challenges of this rapidly changing world. To find them, I ask for your active participation and assistance."

It sounded to me as if the President was looking for one of us average people in *Who's Who*, all right. With his gift of gab, he had finally managed to define that something which makes us All-Stars.

"You, as a leader, are in a position to know and recommend exceptional individuals," his letter continued. "The persons you select should complete the enclosed form and return it to you. I ask that you then attach your comments. My staff will carefully review all recommendations for inclusion in our reservoir of talent from which appointments will be made.

"I will appreciate greatly, Mr. —————, your taking time from your busy schedule to participate in this all-important program.

> Sincerely,
> Richard M. Nixon"

Demonstrating the qualities of creativity and leadership to which the President alluded in his letter, I formed a subcommittee of *Who's Who* members to advise me on my recommendations. This *Who's Who* Task Force, as it came to be called, consisted of such random distinguished listees as hotel executive G. David Schine, lawyer Roy Cohn, civil-rights workers H. Rap Brown and Stokely Carmichael, screen writer Albert Maltz, labor official Jimmy Hoffa, and Professor Owen Lattimore. All were men with experience in or with Washington. Before I could get this diverse group convened, however, the President pulled the rug out from under me. He announced his Cabinet. As chairman of the Task Force, I want to take this opportunity to express our regrets that he saw fit to appoint his Cabinet before our report was in.

What of the Cabinet? By *Who's Who* standards, which obviously carry weight with the President, I have found that two of his appointees are questionable. Despite all the good things the President said about them on television, John N. Mitchell, the Attorney General, and Winton M. Blount, the Postmaster General, had not been considered worthy enough in their other fields of endeavor for the *Who's Who* editors to put them in the book. To be fair about it, Mitchell's name does appear in a slightly smaller volume called *Who's Who in Richard Nixon's Law Firm*, and this probably was recommendation enough.

It was easy to see from the autobiographies of the other eleven Cabinet members in *Who's Who* why they were so attractive. Secretary of Commerce Maurice H. Stans has a D.P.A. degree from prestigious Parsons College. Walter J. Hickel lists the usual qualifications for a Secretary of the Interior: "chmn. bd. Anchorage Natural Gas Co.; dir. Alaska Pipeline Co., Transamerica Title Co." And so forth. On balance, the President was off to a good start.

I am happy to report that he remained vulnerable to the charge of favoritism toward *Who's Who* entries when he got around to the second-level appointees. All of us *Who's Who* people had a drink to celebrate the naming of Elliot Lee Richardson as Under Secretary of State. Not only was he one of us; he was experienced in foreign affairs. As his autobiography in *Who's Who* noted, "Director Salzburg Seminar in Am. Studies." We also rejoiced at the appointment of Daniel Patrick Moynihan, whose success in placing stories about himself in newspapers is cleared up by this line about his first job: "Dir. pub. relations, Internat. Rescue Com., 1954." And, of course, *Who's Who*'s Henry Cabot Lodge was a fine choice for handling the Vietnam negotiations (he already had a white planter's suit).

After several weeks of worrying about the President's problem, it occurred to me that I still hadn't received official notification of my appointment as a presidential adviser. Conducting a random sampling of other *Who's Who* fellows—one of my neighbors in Leonia, New Jersey, is an anthropology professor who had done excellent work in the field of student agitation at Columbia last spring—I was puzzled to learn that the random sample hadn't received his letter either.

My subsequent investigation into what really went on in Operation *Who's Who* was not inspired by pique over this minor technicality. I want to make that crystal clear. Whoever sent out those letters, I was sure at the time, either had been using an earlier edition of the book or was grossly incompetent. I nonetheless felt that the public interest would be best served if I carried my investigation wherever it might lead.

Because listee Herbert G. Klein had repeatedly announced his policy on openness of information since his appointment as Director of Communications for the executive branch, I resolved to call him and find out if *he* had received an invitation to advise the President. My name didn't seem to mean anything to Herb's secretary. "You can look me up in *Who's Who*," I added. After an awkward moment, she said that Mr. Klein wasn't giving any interviews but that his assistant, Paul Costello, was available.

Costello isn't listed in *Who's Who*, but I spoke to him anyway. He said Harry Flemming was in charge of the executive recruiting program. Flemming is in *Who's Who*, in a way. He's listed as the son of Arthur S. Flemming ("mem. Pres. Adv. Com. on Govt. Orgn.,

1953–61"). The head talent hunter's secretary said he was too busy recruiting to talk. But she assured me that his press aide, Copp Collins, could fill me in about the *Who's Who* operation. Collins, it turned out, was tied up and wasn't taking any calls until 5 P.M. When I called back, as instructed, she said Collins had left for the day. Paul Costello, to whom my call was switched, said he'd be able to speak to me the next day. I recognized this innovation in handling the press. It was called the runaround.

After only three more days of my assuring various members of the inner circle that I was not a job seeker, Harry Flemming unexpectedly returned my twelfth call. The only way I can explain this is that a review I had written of two biographies (*Nixon* by Earl Mazo and *Nixon* by Earl Mazo-as-revised-ten-years-later-by-Stephen Hess) had appeared in *The New York Times Book Review* section the day before.

"I'll see if Mr. Kitman is in," I said to Flemming. "He's a very busy man."

Flemming was very open on information about the *Who's Who* thing, which he said was known at the White House officially as "Staff Search and Selection." "It's one of the things the President himself wanted to do," he explained. "The President said he wanted the broadest cross section of people working for him. The problem was laid on our shoulders. We had to reach a lot of people fast. Somebody at a meeting in November brought up *Who's Who*. 'What the hell,' we said. 'Let's see if we can't buy their list of names.' The letter went out to everybody in the book."

**219**

"Are you at liberty to tell me who Mao Tse-tung recommended?" I asked. "He's listed on page 1,404 as 'Chinese Communist polit. leader.'"

Flemming said he had not been aware that the leader of the People's Republic of China was in the book. "But I can assure you," he assured me, "that his recommendation won't carry much weight with *this* administration."

"Did a preponderance of the respondents recommend Walter Hickel?" I asked. "While you're checking the figures, I'd also like to know if the defense-industry people in *Who's Who* were solidly behind David Packard."

He said the administration hadn't had time to analyze the answers yet, although they may do so in the future. He could say that at one point five hundred letters a day were pouring into his office. No attempt had been made to separate the *Who's Who* nominees from the job seekers at large. They had thirty thousand résumés in their files now; he estimated that 60 percent came from the mailing or the publicity about it. "I do remember that Ed Sullivan answered the *Who's Who* letter, but I don't remember who he recommended." Perhaps it was the fellow who wrote the President's speech at the Inaugural Ball.

I asked if a *Who's Who* recommendation carried more weight with the President than, say, a letter from a Republican National Committeeman or a local party leader. "We never think of the answers in that light," Flemming said. "We work on the merit system. If somebody has the qualifications for the job, we slot him."

"Has the President read the book?" I asked. "I wonder what his opinion is of a book of distinguished men which leaves out C. B. Rebozo."

"I bet he'll be listed next year," Flemming observed.

"Was there any special significance in not sending the letter to certain individuals, like, say, myself? Was there a flag on my name in the FBI's copy of the book?"

Flemming insisted that his office had done no sifting, selecting, or screening of any kind. "We bought the list from the *Who's Who* people. They had all the names on a computer tape. It was just an available list of all the prime movers in the country."

This came as something of a surprise to Jackson Martindell, chairman of the board of A. N. Marquis Co., publishers of *Who's Who*. "We never sell our list or aid and abet mail-order schemes of any kind," he said.

*Who's Who*'s management knows that some of the letters were actually mailed by the Nixon staff because there are five intentionally fictitious characters listed in *Who's Who* ("Herbert Kolpitts" and four others). The management calls these dummies burglar-alarm names. Should an enterprising direct-mail salesman try to sell the dignitaries in the book a sweat shirt inscribed "As Listed in *Who's Who*," the sales pitch sent to the burglar-alarm addresses would go directly to the publisher or one of the editors.

The dummies received a copy of Nixon's request for aid, Martindell said, but he had no idea why I didn't get one. "We didn't have anything to do with this operation," he repeated. "Any human being can use our people's names. They're in the public domain."

It is hard to believe that a man like President Nixon, who made a name for himself in politics because of his supersensitivity to undesirables in government, would seek advisers so casually. I don't want to name names or anything like that, but the *Who's Who* fellows include Ken Kesey (who notes in his autobiography that he is "president of Intrepid Trips"), John Rechy and Allen Ginsberg. Between the book's covers can be found a multitude of the intellectuals, alcoholics, sympathizers and homosexuals that the President fought so valiantly to rid us of during a previous stay in Washington. Personally, I'd like to believe that Mr. Nixon's recruiters spent the taxpayers' money buying only those *Who's Who* names which were not on the Attorney General's list.

Whatever the use to which the book was put, it is important to note that *Who's Who* is in its seventieth year and has built up a reputation as a straight shooter. A lot of people still think a prerequisite for being elected to *Who's Who* is a willingness to buy the book. This is not so. The letter informing you of the election results only says that a number of copies are set aside for biographees at a 27 percent discount for a limited time, on a take-it-or-leave-it basis.

Also, as my own listing in Volume 35 proves, fame is not compulsory at *Who's Who*. But holding political office can confer automatic membership. President Nixon originally made the book (Volume 25) the easy way, by being elected to Congress from California in 1946.

All 435 members of the House of Representatives get into *Who's Who* without regard to their notability or prominence in any other respect. Writers and members of other occupations not in *Who's Who*'s "must" categories have to be men of real achievement. We are elected by secret ballot, and we never find out who nominated or seconded us. Not even a brilliant political strategist like Murray Chotiner has figured out how to get in.

Standards for inclusion in *Who's Who* have slipped in recent years, as my own election will attest. I do not plan to stand idly by. My own election and the dangerous inflationary spiral in the number of new members—10,000 in 1968, compared to 200 in 1901—has made me a convert to the movement for tighter standards in the future.

The best place to start the rollback is with congressmen. They should be listed only on the basis of achievement. I would surely include my own congressman, Henry Helstoski (D.-N.J.), for the act of rare political courage he displayed last year: socking his wife while Congress was in session. Others would not be admitted until they, too, had proved their mettle in some way. Throwing the rascals out is admittedly a long-range proposition, yet it is well worth the battle. As we go forward toward final victory, I urge all Americans to close ranks under a banner paraphrased from an earlier Republican era: "What is good for *Who's Who* is good for the country."

# PART FOUR

# WRITER-IN-RESIDENCE

One day in 1967 I read in the paper that a baseball player named Dick Stuart had been given his outright release by the New York Mets. As a free agent, the story explained, the first baseman was now able to make his own deals. Theoretically, anybody could hire a free agent by buying his contract for one dollar. I suddenly realized that an ordinary fan like me could become the first person on his block to own a private major-league ballplayer.

But I wasn't going to spend money to keep Stuart on the bench in front of my house in Leonia, New Jersey, as a mere status symbol. He would play ball every day with my son, the utility outfielder.

Stuart seemed an ideal tutor for my eight-year-old boy because I wanted somebody who wasn't perfect. A young ballplayer can be ruined psychologically by having to measure up to a perfectionist. To err is human, and Stuart's performance in the field proved that he was a regular fellow. His ability to turn a

*Bonus Baby*

**225**

routine ground ball into a sports thrill had earned him the honorary title "Dr. Strangeglove." He liked working with kids, judging by the way he had fielded questions from boys on his *Stump Stuart* pregame TV show.

I was in the market for a major leaguer because of what happened that spring in my son's first season of organized ball. His lifetime baseball record with the Petite Cleaners of the Leonia Skeeter League is not impressive. But scouting reports on my boy were encouraging. The only thing wrong with him, according to neighborhood bird dogs, is his father.

The boner I pulled as manager of his career was believing those psychological articles about the dangers of pushing your boy to star in the little leagues to gratify your own sick needs. When we discussed this in the hot-stove league the previous winter, the Petite Cleaners fathers agreed it was best to let the kids learn the game at their own speed. But on Opening Day, I discovered I was the only enlightened father who hadn't been taking his boy behind the ranch house at night to teach him everything he knew. Well, I would show them how a father *really* can encourage his boy to become a star.

The ex-Met slugger led the league in self-confidence, so I wrote to him in his own language. "Congratulations," began my letter to Stuart at his home in Greenwich, Connecticut, where he was awaiting job offers. "I've decided to pick up your contract for 1967." To prove it was a firm offer, I enclosed my personal check for one dollar.

"Your duties will be to teach my boy the

fundamentals of the game," I wrote, "especially fielding. With a man of your stature tutoring him I see no reason why he can't be ready for the majors within twelve years. None of the little leagues in New Jersey offer instruction in basic economics for young ballplayers, so this is an area where my son really can benefit from your wisdom. He endorsed Petite Cleaners by wearing the company's shirt all season without collecting a penny."

I closed by assuring my new ballplayer that I hoped to sit down with him as soon as possible to talk salary for 1967. "I'm sure we'll be able to work out a fair price for your services," I wrote, "based on the fact that you are currently unemployed. P.S. What size Petite Cleaners shirt will you need?"

Several days later I wrote him a second letter. "I hope your silence doesn't mean you're planning to be a holdout for 1967. Let's stop this haggling and come to terms. Incidentally, my son says that since I'm buying ballplayers, he would prefer Willie Mays."

A few days after that, the phone rang at my house. "It's somebody named Dick Stuart," my wife called out.

"I was out of town and just got your letter," Dick Stuart said. "How much money are you talking about for 1967?"

"Mr. Stuart, I've always been one of your great admirers," I said. "I'm the former president of the Dick Stuart Fan Club of Leonia. I resigned in protest when the club voted to change its name to the Ed Kranepool Fan Club after the Mets released you. . . ."

My ballplayer interrupted, "How much money did you have in mind?"

"I've analyzed your career," I said, stalling while I figured how to explain to my wife that I had bought a major leaguer for the house when we didn't have a maid. "Branch Rickey said a winning player has to be hungry. By working for me, you could work yourself into proper financial condition."

Again Stuart asked about money. "You only hit .218 for the Mets before they dropped you," I said.

"Do you realize I made forty thousand dollars last season?" he asked. "And that a lot of clubs are still after me?"

Obviously Stuart, the master bargainer, was escalating his salary demands by mentioning offers he was getting to jump to Japanese baseball. "Don't think you're the only player who could help my boy," I said, as cold as any major-league magnate dealing with a hireling. "Dee Fondy and Wayne Terwilliger are also free agents."

"Why don't you teach the kid how to play ball yourself?" Stuart suggested.

"And have the kid hate me because I pushed him into baseball?" I asked. "I did show him how to take a cut at the ball before one game. He struck out every time. But that was just his way of rebelling against his father."

"Nobody can teach your boy how to play," Stuart said.

"Are you trying to tell me my son is hopeless?"

"I mean all you can do is *show* kids the fundamentals of the game. Not even Ted Williams could *teach* an eight-year-old. A kid has to mature first."

To break the impasse, I made a concrete offer. "I'm sure your accountant would prefer a deferred-payment deal. I'll give you fifty percent of the bonus the kid gets when he signs with a major-league club, plus the Cadillac."

Stuart shrewdly avoided saying no—and he left the door open by telling me to get in touch as soon as I figured out what I could pay him next year.

One solution to the high cost of owning a private major leaguer was to lease him to other fathers who wanted their sons to sit at the feet of a master. I had two days of Stuart's time booked for 1967 when I read that my ballplayer had been lured away by a cartel of West Coast oil and real-estate tycoons called the Los Angeles Dodgers.

Connie Mack once said, "You can't win them all." But I wasn't discouraged. I had a hunch Stuart might soon be a free agent again, and my strategy now was to play a waiting game. I wrote Stuart a letter congratulating him on his new job with the Dodgers. "Just a reminder that my offer still holds for next season. Spring training begins on April 1 at Sylvan Park in Leonia. I don't want to influence your decision, but Sylvan Park has a short left-field wall."

*A Frank Sex*
*Talk, as Told*
*to the*
*Cosmo Girl*

I've been reading all the sociological studies in CosMOPOLITAN about how to meet interesting men. It's a subject I don't have to know anything about. Still, I've noticed that the writers haven't mentioned one of the more highly developed forms of the species yet. The most exciting, fascinating men in America today are the political satirists, and that is why I am glad I am one.

The problem is: There are only a handful of professional political satirists in the country today (although there are many amateurs in government). Frankly, I feel guilty turning you on to them. There just aren't enough to meet the fantastic demand.

*How do you meet a fabulous satirist?*

Once a week (usually on Thursdays) they arrive by bus in New York City.

It's a mean, sneaky, underhand thing to do to all those girls who don't read this magazine. But I'm going to give you some idea of how easy and convenient it is to meet a satirist. The buses from Leonia, New Jersey, most likely to carry satirists arrive in New York at 8:25 and 8:47 A.M.

*How do you recognize one of these rare, interesting men?*

Your average satirist is five feet ten, weighs 175 pounds, has dewy (or watery) brown eyes, and wears a fashionably ragged Burberry trenchcoat (with an Abercrombie & Fitch label). If you still can't pick him out of the crowd of less-than-great men in the Port Authority Bus Terminal, he's the one wearing glasses.

**230**

*What does a political satirist do in town, in*

*case you're not near the bus terminal around 9 A.M.?*

He goes to his office.

*What does a political satirist do in the office?*

He says good morning to the other political satirists.

Then he takes his week's phone calls. Sometimes there aren't any of these. When someone does call, it is usually a young writer asking how to break into this glamorous field. The professional political satirist assures the young gifted kids on the way up there are no openings in the field for new satirists, and probably won't be any for twenty-five years.

If you're lucky enough to get to meet a satirist someday, and he really is knocked out by your appearance, he'll let you watch him while he works at his craft. This consists of reading *The New York Times* and clipping out all the funny things the congressmen, cabinet officers and Mayor Lindsay said the day before. You can't imagine how groovy this can be without having done it once. Then he knocks off for lunch.

*Where do the go-go political satirists lunch, in case you still haven't crossed their paths?*

At their desks.

This is a rotten trick to pull on the other girls. But you're interested in results, not moral victories. So don't tell anybody where you heard this: the best way to nonchalantly meet a political satirist is to get a part-time job as a take-out girl at Shelley's Luncheonette or the Victoria Delicatessen, delivering lunches. A political satirist in Room 702 may invite you to have lunch with him. Even if he doesn't, it's outdoor work and the tips are good.

**231**

*Isn't there any way you can meet a political satirist out of the office?*

Well, a lot of satirists have a country place where they sometimes go.

*Why do so many political satirists choose to live outside New York?*

Primarily to get away from the mad social whirl of the city. It's less distracting working in the basement of a house in the suburbs. One satirist I know only comes into the city one day a week.

*Are there any special things a girl should know about before trying to visit a political satirist in his country hideaway?*

Yes. You should know about his wife.

*Oh! Do political satirists tend to be married?*

The truth is that at the present time there are no successful political satirists in this country who are unmarried. Why this is so, I'm not sure. One theory is that they are exceptionally attractive human beings.

*With the technical difficulties you've mentioned in such detail so far, how does a girl go about meeting and wooing a political satirist of her very own?*

I don't know. That's why I am writing this article about what I feel is a very serious social problem.

I suppose I might as well confess that I haven't been writing entirely *objectively* about the whole field of political satirists. Everything I've been trying to pass off here as general information is actually autobiographical. And, as you might have guessed, what I am *really* hinting at is that I'd like one of those girls who want to meet *men* to want to meet *me*. I guess you could say that I *live* for the day when I will meet a COSMOPOLITAN girl, *That* COSMOPOL-ITAN Girl! Political satirist that I am, I also know that, somewhere, a COSMOPOLITAN Girl is dying to meet me.

I've had these wild dreams before. There was the time I wanted to meet the White Rock Girl. But nothing ever came of it.

I don't usually think about meeting strange women. My nine-to-five day in town is so filled with important work—like researching a book I'm doing now on the first George Washington presidential campaign, titled *The Making of the Prefident 1789*—I just don't have time for that kind of nonsense.

My attitude began to change last month when a COSMOPOLITAN editor called and asked if I wanted to meet the COSMOPOLITAN Girl. "What for?" I asked suspiciously. It sounded like a blind date, since I didn't know the girl. I was very excited, however, and told the editor I would be free for drinks at 9 A.M. at the Port Authority Bus Terminal cocktail lounge and bowling alley, a really "in" place. All she had in mind, I learned, was my reading a series of ads about the COSMOPOLITAN Girl that had been appearing in *The New York Times, Women's Wear Daily*, and *Time* magazine and telling the literary world what I thought of her.

I dug the COSMOPOLITAN Girl right away. When I hinted that I wanted to get to know her better, the editor sent me the last twelve issues of COSMOPOLITAN. I didn't realize what an obsession the COSMO Girl (to use my pet nickname for her) had become in my life since then, until I looked back in my diary. Strictly speaking, it isn't a diary; we professional writers call this place where we put down our true

**233**

secret thoughts a "journal." To protect my reputation in the literary establishment if it is ever published, it will be under my pseudonym, "Name Withheld." The observations on this super girl began appearing the day I read the ads.

*SUNDAY*

DEAR JOURNAL:

Every red-blooded American man has his own reasons for liking the COSMO Girl. Take this fellow named Allen who told *all* in *The Times:* he admired her because she wasn't so simple as Cream of Wheat. "I think that what he was talking about," the COSMO Girl in the ad explained, "is that one night I'm a long-haired island girl (with dewy make-up to match) and next night I'm an East Sixties hostess (with two rows of fake eyelashes and gold glitter on my eyelids)." Well, that says a lot about Allen, but it would confuse the hell out of me.

What I like most about the COSMO Girl is that she is good for the country. "At last count," one COSMO Girl reported in her ad, "I have twelve shades of eyeshadow, six lip glossers, five hairpieces, and two facial saunas." I don't even know what a facial sauna is, but I am sure all that buying and traveling around they do helps the economy. If the COSMO Girls ever lost interest in improving themselves, the dollar would collapse.

All I want to do when I finally meet a COSMO Girl is shake her hand, maybe slap her on the back, and tell her to keep up the good work.

So, my motives are quite honorable.

*MONDAY*

. . . As sound as my reasoning is on paper, it

wasn't easy explaining all of this to Carol [the author's wife]; for some reason, I think she feels threatened by the COSMO Girl. I found some doodlings on the July 1968 issue: a hangman's noose drawn around the pretty cover girl's neck. The doodle read, SHE LOOKS HAPPY, BUT SHE'S REALLY MISERABLE.

*TUESDAY*

. . . Why don't I just work late Thursday night, have a drink with the COSMO Girl, tell her how much I admire what she's doing to make the country economically sound, and not get Carol involved.

I know why. Professional satirists never have to work late at the office. Nothing satirical happens at night. . . .

*WEDNESDAY*

Rough draft of a classified ad for the *Saturday Review*'s personals column:

WRITER, 38, intsd. meeting COSMO GIRL. Age open; for brief conversation only, maybe ten-minute gourmet dinner.

*THURSDAY*

It started when I came home from a hard day at the office in New York. I gathered from what my wife was saying that she thought I had been sleeping with somebody on the ten-minute bus ride across the George Washington Bridge. I found last May's issue of COSMOPOLITAN in the kitchen. She had been reading one of those great public-service features, "How to Be a Lady While Dating a Married Man" [May 1968, COSMO].

Nancy Weber wrote that, I explained. "You know Nancy, she's probably only kidding around again."

**235**

We had met Nancy when I was running for the GOP presidential nomination, as a Lincoln Republican, in 1964. She was the editor of the Sarah Lawrence newspaper and had arranged a rally so I could speak to the political activists in Bronxville. It was a memorable chilly afternoon. The students asked what my position as a presidential candidate was on Herman Hesse. "I know his brother, Rudolph," I remember saying, flabbergasted. One of the girls said Nancy had dragged her out of her sickbed—she had the flu—to hear me speak about the principles of Jefferson upon which the Republican Party was based. Or was it Jackson? I looked down in embarrassment. She was barefoot. No wonder those Sarah Lawrence girls are so often sick. Nancy apologized afterward for her classmates' acting as if they had never heard of the Republican politicians I was satirizing at the time: Rockefeller, Goldwater, Nixon and Harold Stassen.

Over the years we'd see Nancy at cocktail parties and have a good laugh over that political disaster. As far as I was concerned, I lost the nomination at Sarah Lawrence. We'd see more and more of Nancy, in the sense that she always seemed to be wearing less and less at parties. "She's quite a kidder," I kept reminding Carol.

*FRIDAY*

Carol came home with ten dollars' worth of make-up from Bloomingdale's. That seemed odd.

*SATURDAY*

An unusual thing happened tonight. Carol served dinner in a topless dress.

**236**

*SUNDAY*

Carol said she had been reading Cosmo again and had been very moved by one of their socio-economic studies, "How Not to Get Dumped on *His* Way Up" [October 1968, Cosmo].

She also asked me how my affair with Nancy Weber was going.

*MONDAY*

Carol said she had decided to take a part-time job as a scientific researcher so she would be more interesting as a woman. She goes to work with Masters and Johnson at the Washington University of St. Louis Sex Laboratory next Thursday.

I told her that I thought she was overreacting and it wasn't very funny.

*TUESDAY*

Carol said she didn't want to stand in the way of my meeting the Cosmo Girl any more. She was giving me my freedom. She had also decided to give me the three children, the house she's always hated, and my parents. I could write to her at the New York Athletic Club, until she found her own little apartment in the East Sixties.

She batted her new false eyelashes at me and went back to reading "I've Been Loved by Men Worth Loving" by Nancy Weber [November 1968, Cosmo].

*WEDNESDAY*

I sat down this morning and coldly analyzed my disintegrating marriage. What was in it for me, anyway? I'm getting sick and tired of having a woman who respects me; treats me like a king; laughs at my private jokes; doesn't complain about reading my manuscripts and improves them with her editing; is a great

**237**

cook; a warm and compassionate good person who loves and adores me. Women like that are a dime a dozen.

The problem with us was that bundle of Cos-MOPOLITANS sitting on my desk and inflaming her every morning.

*THURSDAY*

I left the seditious COSMOPOLITANS on the bus, accidentally, this morning.

So I won't meet a COSMO Girl. Worse things have happened to me, although I can't think of any right now.

---

## Confessions of a Podiatrist Watcher

When somebody calls out frantically "Is there a podiatrist in the house?" I can usually step in and help out in the emergency. Most often the medical problem is that the girl's feet are killing her. "Get those shoes off immediately," I say firmly to the girl's distraught escort. "That poor woman's feet need to breathe." Nine times out of ten, my advice works. The patient feels better within seconds.

I learned so much about podiatry by studying at the feet of six of the greatest foot doctors in New York City on a generous grant from *Cosmopolitan*. The specialists I consulted ranged from the brilliant—but unknown outside the profession—Dr. H.C.C. (I will use initials because it is against the medical profession's ethics to advertise) to the current fair-haired boy of the field, Dr. I.S., the genius who has been widely written up in the press recently for his work on a case of a most delicate nature. Who, you may ask, *is* Dr. S.? Only the gifted man who worked on the feet of Jackie

O., the wife of the Greek shipping magnate (we might as well go all the way protecting people's dignity). More about Dr. S. and Jackie O. later.

All of these podiatrists, needless to say, also learned a lot studying at *my* feet.

Frankly, I wasn't wild about the idea of going to podiatrists at first. I hate doctors. "Well, if you have cold feet," the editor said, "we'll give the assignment to George Plimpton." My professional pride was stirred. "Plimpton can't write an objective piece on the subject," I explained. "He has athlete's feet."

My feet, on the other hand, had carried me on twenty-mile hikes in the Army. They once had won a mambo contest. They had done the Louvre in fourteen minutes flat, a world record. What did I have to fear?

My wife explained what I had to fear. "Those editors must be foot fetishists. There's nothing that thrills these people more than finding an innocent and turning him on to their barbarous practices." I decided to run the risk anyway. More than my fear of doctors, I have a pathological fear of missing out on the "in" sexual thing.

I had caught breast, buttocks, and thigh fetishes covering stories for *Playboy* (this explains why I sometimes run amok at cocktail parties, but only when I encounter a woman who has any of those sex symbols). A foot fetish seemed like an especially good thing to have. It gives a man more scope as a human being.

American men tend to be specialists, being attracted to women who have one perfect part of the body. As a result they often find nobody good enough to talk to at cocktail parties and

**239**

stand around looking bored. But generalists, like the Italians, can see something beautiful in any woman—a well-turned wrist, a plump earlobe, a shapely toe. Their reputation as great lovers stems from this. Women respond favorably to genuine looks of appreciation. And even if a woman has nothing else going for her, she usually has a pair of feet.

All the podiatrists seemed to welcome the chance to discuss the romance of feet with me, as well as the latest scientific theories, such as the relationship between a woman's cold feet and her warm heart (it is a fact that women's feet are colder than men's, I learned: "The normal skin temperature of a woman's foot is 66–80 degrees; a man's is 72–84"). As a group, podiatrists, I found, tend to be extroverts. They are also a little shorter and paunchier than nonpodiatrists, and resemble dentists. (Dr. L.R., a female podiatrist, wore sensible shoes.)

The podiatrists I studied for this story fell into several categories, the most avant-garde being members of the school which treats the foot as only part of the human body. Going to one of these men, like Doctor J., can be an emotionally exhausting experience, as this excerpt from my notebook indicates:

Q. Mr. K., how do you feel about your feet?

A. How do I what?

Q. I'm sorry to embarrass you this way. But your feet are the most important thing you have in the world. Ask anybody who doesn't have them. What are your inner feelings concerning your feet?

A. Well, since you ask, Dr. J., I've always been hostile to my feet.

Q. Good! What seems to be the source of the emotional difficulty?

A. I think my first metatarsal doesn't get along with the other metatarsals. It's been that way since I was a kid. I think they rub each other the wrong way.

Q. Hmm. I'm sorry to press you on this. But for too long podiatry has been just a mechanical thing.

A. I understand perfectly. I've always wanted to tell somebody about my rotten feet. They don't respect authority. Often, I want to go one way and they go the other.

And so forth. As my answers reveal, I found it hard to take this type of podiatrist seriously. It may be that I was *blocking*, possibly because I secretly thought there might be something *to* the relationship between feet and psyche. (As a boy I was often told that my brains were in my feet.) You, however, might find baring your soul this way a cheap form of therapy.

The second type of podiatrist I encountered is the lecher who actually wants to look at your feet. They even ask you to disrobe.

When I learned of this practice, I mentioned in passing to a podiatrist that there seemed to be a lot of unnecessary undressing going on in doctors' offices today. (My wife had told me a few weeks earlier about a general practitioner in New Jersey who asked her to disrobe for a common cold. "He's probably doing a research paper on the average number of breasts women have," she said.) "How do you handle

**241**

the problem of women who refuse to undress?" I asked a podiatrist I shall call Dr. C.

"I assure them all podiatrists require that a patient, prior to a thorough examination of the feet, take off her shoes and stockings."

There are no screens for disrobing in podiatrists' offices, however, which creates a problem for the modest girl who may be wearing panty hose. But not in the eyes of a podiatrist.

"To us," Dr. C. said, "a woman is only a pair of feet. That's all we see."

Dr. C. described an interesting case. He had instructed Miss N. to take her shoes and stockings off, and left the examining room to attend another woman (Miss B.) in the adjoining cubicle. When he returned, he found Miss N. waiting for him naked, *except* for her shoes and stockings. Regaining his senses, he rushed out of the room and told his assistant to go in there and warn the woman to put her clothes back on and take her shoes and stockings *off*.

"Do you get many exhibitionists?"

"Fortunately, I've only had one case like that in my eleven years of practice," Dr. C. said. "Apparently, the woman was a Hungarian émigrée who had a language difficulty. Thinking about it later, it was funny. The scene reminded me of my pre-induction physical."

It didn't seem very wholesome to me that a man could look at a woman and see only her feet. "Tell me, Doctor," I said, using the aforementioned Dr. J.'s technique, "is there any psychological quirk that makes a man go into podiatry, like the drives that make a man go into gynecology, proctology, or psychology?"

"When I was in college," Dr. C. confessed, "my feet always hurt."

242

Another type of podiatrist you run into is the one who wants to feel your feet. All over. Some of these podiatrists seem constitutionally unable to keep their hands to themselves. You can try to hide your feet by sitting on them or putting them under the chair. Even if you assume the lotus position—while the podiatrist is trying to relax you by talking about the high cost of air-conditioning an office, the stock market, or whatever else is on the average doctor's mind—he will be trying to get your feet into his hands.

One of the most common excuses for pressing the flesh of the foot is taking your pulse. In the foot? Apparently this is an index of good or bad circulation.

Dr. K. remembered a case where a woman hit the ceiling every time he touched her feet. "Can you give me all the details of that case," I said, writing furiously.

"She was ticklish," he observed in a clinical manner. "What was odd about her behavior, of course, is that generally the threshold of a woman's nerve response is very low. Men are much more ticklish than women. We overcome this problem by never touching the foot lightly." This explains the podiatrist's famous heavy touch (the medical term is *manu morte*).

Do women like having their feet treated roughly? I asked podiatrists of all schools. They unanimously agreed women are masochists when it comes to their feet. "This is the only way you can explain the way they torture them every day," one podiatrist said. "It's simple mathematics. When you try to put five toes in the space designed for three, you have to learn how to live with pain."

Discussions about indecent footwear inevitably led to the nitty-gritty of podiatry: the aberrant behavior of patients. Nothing I had read in Krafft-Ebing prepared me for the case of the woman who always wore two pairs of stockings. "When I called this to her attention," Dr. C. reported, "she said, 'Doesn't everybody?' "

People who bite their toenails are rare today. "This is what we call Hackett's phenomenon," Dr. C. observed, "and can be cured by wearing your shoes and socks in bed, when the desire is most likely to arise."

Man to man, I asked Dr. C. if he had ever seen a really beautiful foot—one that, so to speak, turned him on, if he knew what I meant. I had the feeling that he was about to terminate the interview by calling the police. But he broke the tension by smiling.

"Ahh, you mean the so-called *pretty* foot. I treat many of the foot models who star in commercials." He didn't have any pictures that we could pore over together, but he said I'd recognize the feet if I saw them on television. "It's the high arch with the long toes . . . unmistakable."

He sketched it on a prescription pad. I said that I had never seen such a beautiful foot. "It's actually a very weak foot," he said. "All right to date feet like these, but you don't want to marry them. They're always at the podiatrist. The high arch drops as easily as a soufflé. These girls don't have the normal fat pad on the bottom of the foot that acts as a shock absorber. It's hard to fit them with shoes. They're especially prone to traumatic arthritis and heel spurring. Yet this is the foot photographers go wild over."

The one point podiatrists raised that seemed to fly in the face of facts is that women are braver than men, at least on the podiatrist's couch. Dr. C. said he had one patient, a police lieutenant decorated six times in gun battles, who passed out every time he visited the office. "The first time it happened," Dr. C. recalled, "I was very disconcerted. But now that we know what to expect, it doesn't upset the routine of the office so much."

While all of these scholarly discussions were going on, I observed podiatrists as they examined *other* feet, but I didn't once let them look at mine. I was saving myself for Dr. S., who, I had heard through the grapevine (the literary editor of the *New Republic*), was too busy these days to talk to reporters—particularly since he had been linked to Jackie O. So I went to Dr. S. with the cover story that my feet were tired from doing too many Greek dances at wedding feasts.

The great Dr. S. has an office in the lobby of a once-fashionable skyscraper on Seventh Avenue in the heart of the garment center. Next door is a barbershop. As I lay reclining on the podiatrist's couch, a kind of dentist's or barber's chair, Dr. S. observed sourly, "There may be a nonmedical problem involved. Perhaps your dancing partners are boring."

He scraped his thumb against my sole as he spoke and I almost went out of control. "You

**245**

have it," he said. "Have what?" I asked nervously. "Babinski's reflex. Your toes curl when I scrape the bottom of the foot."

While he fooled around like that, I made small talk. "What are Jackie O.'s feet really like?" Suddenly, the double-chinned doctor's head shot up. This must have been the Jackie O. reflex. "I mean, did she have her feet shortened or anything?"

He said he couldn't tell me about her feet. "But I won't tell her about your feet, either. I think I know what your problem is, but first I want to take some X-rays."

There must be some mistake, I explained as he took the X-rays—two sets, top and side. "There's nothing really wrong with my feet. I have weak ankles when I skate, but who doesn't?"

"Your difficulty comes from the fact that you're unbalanced," he said. My wife has been telling me that for years, but I didn't have to come all the way into New York from New Jersey to hear anything like that from a *foot* doctor. "Sit down, Mr. K.," Dr. S. went on. "Eighty percent of the American people have bad feet and don't know it. For years you've been walking around on unbalanced feet. But it's nothing we can't fix. All we have to do is rebuild your fulcrum."

"Are you trying to tell me my fulcrum is shot?" I said, to let him know that I was knowledgeable when it came to podiatry. "First we'll have to make plaster casts of your feet," Dr. S. went on, "then we make corrective devices which can be slipped in and out of your shoes. Six or seven visits. Only $155."

I must have turned as white as plaster of

Paris. "It's not that serious," he said. "I've seen far worse cases of imbalance. The trouble is that one imbalance can lead to another." At this time I was only worried about how a man who had perfect feet would justify an expenditure of $155 for a new fulcrum on his expense account ("I was mistaken for a member of Jackie O.'s jet set," I fancied myself explaining to the magazine's comptroller). Concluded the doctor: "Of course, you'll have to learn how to walk again."

"I've heard enough out of you, Dr. S.," I announced with the authority of a *Women's Wear Daily* reporter. "They're *your* feet," Dr. S. said with contempt; "if you want to endanger them. . . . Do you mind if I at least cut your toenails? They look awful." After writing a check for $25—nobody walks out on Dr. S. without paying his bill—I managed to escape to Seventh Avenue.

The next type of podiatrist I ran into was the specialist who tries to cover up the wrong diagnosis of the first specialist. This is a fairly common practice in the medical profession. I remember reading a copy of the doctor's bible, *Medical Economics*, which had an article about what surgeons should do in case they discover a sponge left over from a previous operation. "First," the article cautioned, "there is no need to alarm the patient by informing him of your discovery."

In Dr. B.H.A.'s opinion, my condition was even worse than Dr. S. had indicated. "What you have is a shortened hamstring muscle. Look, you can't even grip your toes on my fingers." Of course I couldn't; I was too weak

**247**

from all the bad news I had been hearing about my feet that day.

"The toes grab when you walk," Dr. A., my sixth podiatrist, lectured. "This increases the circulation of the blood. In effect, what a man with healthy feet has is a second heart in his feet, which helps do the heavy work for the old man upstairs." He tapped at the left side of my chest with his finger. "It may not affect you today, but a couple of years from now . . . you could go like *that*." He snapped his fingers. My heart fell to my feet.

Dr. A. told me he had worked on many famous people's feet. In a nostalgic mood, he showed me the plaster casts of each dignitary, lifting them from a pile in the corner of his office. Making such a foot mold, he said, also was the first step in my own treatment. It would cost only $65.

So I agreed to have my feet cast in plaster of Paris. It wasn't only that every step I had taken since leaving Dr. S.'s office in the garment center had caused me great agony. Or that I feared the next podiatrist I went to would recommend a foot transplant. The real reason was that the plaster casts were pure pop art. Dr. A.'s work, I could see, was as sensitive as George Segal's sculpture. Put the plaster-feet molds on a pedestal in a living room, and a member of the opposite sex could worship at them. Such an ingenious device for turning a conversation to feet!

I don't know if I've been lucky enough to have caught a foot fetish from visiting so many podiatrists' offices. But I certainly have a fixation. Any man who can look at feet with sin-

cere interest, as I can, has to be way ahead of
the other fellows.

---

In 1967, I received what appeared to be the
biggest assignment of my career. The editors of
*Saturday Evening Post* sent me a classified ad
from *The Wall Street Journal* announcing that
the Turkish government was offering to sell a
surplus battleship named the *Sultan Yavuz
Selim*. (I later learned the Turks called it by
the diminutive *Yavuz*, much the way Americans refer to the U.S.S. *Missouri* as the *Mo*.)
The *Yavuz* was moored at the Poyraz wharf,
the Golcuk naval base, in Turkey, waiting
for the highest bidder.

The only instruction the editors sent along
with the clipping was, "Buy it."

I had never written anything about the sea
like Ancient Mariner Herman Wouk. It was a
great tribute to my reputation as a wheeler
and dealer.

My wife had another explanation. "Every
time they get a crazy idea, they give it to you.
When are you going to grow up and stop acting
out their childhood fantasies?"

"You're right, dear," I said. "I'm not going
to act out anybody's fantasies any more. From
here on out, I'm acting out my own fantasies."

You can imagine how excited I was about
buying a battleship on an expense account.
Visions of the petty-cash voucher I'd turn in
after the story was finished danced before my
eyes:

*Remember
the Yavuz!*

**249**

Telephone calls: 50 cents
Postage: 16 cents
Two cups of Turkish coffee, plus tip: $1.20
One used battleship: $985,000 (or whatever low figure I brought the ship in at, after a haggling session with the Turks over coffee)

I didn't know what the magazine wanted a used battleship for. Maybe they were planning to get involved in a circulation war or something. But I couldn't sleep that night, thinking of all the things I could do once my ship had finally come in.

All the "in" creative people in the New York area were moving to the West Side. I've stuck it out in the suburbs of New Jersey because of my fear of the violence in the city's streets. A lot of people already were living happily on houseboats moored off Sausalito, in the San Francisco area. Perhaps I could find peace of mind living in a battleship moored in the Hudson Harbor Boat Basin, off Manhattan's West Seventy-ninth Street, only a few blocks down the road from the Dakota, the exclusive residence of Lauren Bacall, Jason Robards, Betty Friedan and the other people I wanted for neighbors.

On the short walk from the IRT subway to the boat basin, it wouldn't be any trouble for my wife, stationed in the *Yavuz*'s gun turrets, to keep me covered. At the first sign of a mugger, she could let him have it.

By my wife's salty language when I woke her up to tell her that we would soon be moving to the West Side, I got the impression she didn't think *her* ship had come in yet. "Now hear this," I announced happily a few minutes later. "Frank Sinatra will stay at our place the next time he comes to town, once he hears we've got a yacht the size of the *Yavuz*."

More salty language. I guess the reason she was so upset was the thought of all the brass she'd have to polish to get the house ready for guests. The *Yavuz* was a little big for a houseboat. I explained that we could rent space to the Bill Buckleys, the Jules Feiffers, the Norman Mailers, a nice Negro family like the Ralph Bunches, and anybody else worried about the next long hot summer in New York. Then we'd have the first ironclad apartment-houseboat in town.

But what if she didn't change her tone of voice by the time my battleship arrived? Well, the magazine article could turn into something bigger, like a nonfiction novel titled *Mutiny on the Yavuz*. The trouble with that idea was that there wouldn't be a mutiny, because once I got the feel of the battleship's bridge under me, I wouldn't have to waste time reasoning with the crew. Anyone guilty of insubordination would spend the summer in the brig with my children.

I continued thinking about the advantages of owning a battleship. Suppose the right-wing groups were right about the Communists' planning to take over American homes. The *Yavuz* would be a more effective deterrent than a rifle in the family fallout shelter. A neighbor had been asking me to join the local Just-a-Minutemen group. With my own battleship, I probably could get a commission as an ensign or a lieutenant j.g. in the citizens' navy.

Last, but not least, I wanted the ship so that

I could finally pay homage to the section of Brooklyn where I first fell in love with the sea as a boy. My plan was to rechristen the Turkish ship the *Sheepshead Bey*.

Through private sources I had developed in my years as a free-lance writer, I quietly began investigating the *Yavuz*, to find out what she was worth. At the New York Public Library, the librarian suggested I look up the *Yavuz* in *Jane's Fighting Ships*. It turned out she wasn't just an ordinary battleship but, until deactivated recently, the *flagship* of the entire Turkish navy. Designed by Professor Kretsschner, built in the famed Hamburg shipyards of Blohm and Voss in 1911, she was commissioned the *Linienschiff Kreuzer* (dreadnought) *Goeben*. The pride of Kaiser Wilhelm's fleet, she made front-page headlines in *The New York Times* the first day of World War I.

First Lord of the Admiralty Winston Churchill ordered the British fleet to seize the *Goeben* at all costs. From Sicily, across the Mediterranean, through the Dardanelles, into the Sea of Marmara, the *Goeben* outraced the British until she ran out of coal outside the city limits of Constantinople (Istanbul). The Royal Navy was cheated of its prize by a remarkable naval maneuver executed by the Ottoman Empire (as neutral Turkey was then known). As the British dreadnoughts H.M.S. *Indomitable*, H.M.S. *Indefatigable* and six other warships steamed in for the kill, the *Goeben* suddenly ran up the crescent and star of the Imperial Ottoman Navy. Wearing new fezzes, the German sailors rushed to the deck and waved neutrally at the British.

The ship had been sold on the spot—presumably at what merchants call a "distress sale" price—to the Turks, something that had never happened before in the midst of a naval battle.

"I can't go through with it," I told one of the editors who had given me the assignment. "An illustrious ship like that shouldn't be allowed to fall into the hands of an infidel like myself. I'll start a campaign to collect pennies from Turkish-American school children to save the *Yavuz*. I'll try to find a home for it in a museum so its grandeur can be preserved. But don't make me buy it."

An infidel himself, he moved up my deadline for the article one week.

Before plunging into the used-battleship market, I checked to make sure I wouldn't get arrested for violating the Sullivan Law in New York. "There are laws against carrying concealed weapons," explained Mel Wulf, director of the New York chapter of the American Civil Liberties Union, "but this doesn't seem to be a concealed weapon. There are laws against buying machine guns, but there's nothing on the statute books against buying battleships—yet."

I asked him what he meant by "yet." He said Congress was studying new firearms-control legislation, in view of the recent assassination boom. "But don't worry. The National Rifle Association will back you to the hilt on this thing. They're against any law that infringes on the constitutional right of the citizen to bear arms." When our founding fathers wrote that guarantee into the Bill of Rights, it obviously wasn't just so the jet set could go fox hunting in New Jersey. The ACLU lawyer asked to be third mate on the *Yavuz*.

"PROCEEDING FULL SPEED AHEAD ON BATTLE-SHIP ASSIGNMENT," I wired the magazine collect. "PLEASE ALERT BOOKKEEPING DEPARTMENT."

J. P. Morgan once said that if you have to ask how much a boat costs, you can't afford it. So I didn't discuss price in answering the Turkish Ministry of Finance's ad. "Does it have a Turkish bath?" I asked the man the switchboard operator at the Turkish embassy in Washington referred me to. Zeki Toker, Chairman of the Board of Counselors for Economic Affairs, explained he didn't know the plumbing specifications. Since I was the first American to inquire about this "wonderful ship," he still hadn't translated the specification sheets from Ankara. "But I do know it is 19,950,000 pounds."

I told him I didn't care how much the ship weighed.

"That is the asking price in Turkish pounds," explained the used-battleship salesman. The negotiations had started sooner than I had anticipated.

It has been said that in the history of doing business with the Turks, the customer has never come out on top. But I haggled, anyway. "My people have authorized me to buy the *Yavuz*," I explained after laughing at his absurd list price. "Not the whole Turkish navy."

"Tell me," Mr. Toker asked, "for what purpose do you want this wonderful ship?"

At that moment, I was lost in another one of my Mittyesque reveries about the *Yavuz*. I saw myself sailing the battleship, with my wife

254

below decks stoking coal into the boilers, bravely into the harbor of Ocean Beach, a resort on Fire Island where I vacationed before I became a free-lance writer and could no longer afford summer vacations. From the bridge of the ship, I was shouting through a megaphone at Ocean Beach's trembling mayor: "Hand over your women and your money—or I'll blast this island out of the water."

But I told Mr. Toker: "For fishing."

I'll admit I wasn't being completely honest with him, but, as it turned out, he wasn't being honest with me, either.

I had an appointment to see Mr. Toker at the Turkish embassy the next day. But first I called an expert who might know something more about the *Yavuz* than was listed in *Jane's Fighting Ships*, 1923. "If they haven't sold it in the bazaar at Istanbul yet," explained the military attaché at the Greek embassy, "there must be something wrong with it." He wasn't as objective a source as Consumers Union, but the information at least put me on guard.

"Before I buy the ship," I asked Mr. Toker in the embassy's conference room the next day, "would your government mind if I sent my own mechanic to look it over?"

He looked down at the Oriental rug on the floor, then at the gleaming scimitar on the wall over my head. For the next few minutes, he told me what a wonderful ship the *Yavuz* was, how it had led the bombardment against Sevastopol and Odessa in 1914—the sneak attacks that had brought Turkey into the war against Russia. "We are anti-Communists, too," he added.

**255**

"But is the ship still afloat?"

"For such an old ship, it is very well preserved. Everything is still on board."

"Good. What days do you deliver to Leonia, New Jersey?"

He gazed out of the window at the Potomac River for a long while. "Well, I wouldn't mind driving it home myself," I explained. "We can take a spin around Cyprus, test-fire the guns—"

"It makes no steam," he interrupted. On further questioning, the embassy official said he had forgotten to mention one thing: the boilers had been removed. A few moments later, he added that the *Yavuz*'s anchor and shackle were not included in the sale, either. And the barometer and steering compass were missing. That reminded him of something else: "She has no steering wheel."

"But at least she still has a rudder?" I asked hopefully. After all, who wants to buy a battleship without at least driving it around the block, even if it has to be towed?

He shook his head sadly. "No."

"And what of the guns?"

"The six big guns are still on board, yes."

If I had been Lawrence of Arabia instead of Marvin of New Jersey, I would have shot the used-battleship salesman on the spot as a profiteer. *Jane's Fighting Ships* had listed ten big (11-inch) guns, twenty-four smaller guns, all made by Krupp. I assumed the four torpedo tubes, which I really needed for laundry chutes and garbage disposal, had also disappeared into the bazaar, and I adjusted my bid downward again. "Can this wonderful ship at least be towed home, where my people can get it running again?"

"Maybe yes," Mr. Toker said, lighting a Turkish cigarette. "Maybe no."

"You mean you expect me to buy a ship that might sink as soon as I drive away from the dock? I don't think my friends at the Chase Manhattan Bank would give anybody a boat loan on such a risky proposition."

If that happened, he shrugged, it would be the will of Allah. "After you own your ship," he added, "you examine it. Your frogman can do this easily in some other port."

Maybe that *was* the way people bought battleships today. I was still ready to buy the *Yavuz*; after all, it wasn't my money. Then I started reading over the conditions of the sale, which included:

Article I, paragraph 2: The foreigners who would enter in the ship area because of their job should present the letter issued from their embassy, certifying they are trustworthy. It is forbidden to bring wireless-set, telescope, camera and cinematographic apparatus into this area; to take a photograph; and to sketch; and to observe the area through telescope or such other means as this.

I asked Mr. Toker a simple question: "What does *Yavuz* mean in English?"

He said, "A jolly fellow." Unfortunately, *The New York Times* of 1914 had given the word a slightly different interpretation, reporting it meant "The Grim."

By this time, I was really worried. I was losing faith in the salesman, and with a battleship it's not like a car that you can kick the tires and look under the hood to make him think you know something. The *Yavuz* might even be in worse shape than Mr. Toker had let on. I wasn't going to fly to the Poyraz wharf

**257**

at the Golcuk naval base and go down with a ship just to get a story. The angle I chose instead played up how I had saved the magazine from a major naval and financial disaster by not buying a glorified piece of junk like the *Yavuz*. A few weeks later, an editor called and said that was some story I wrote about the Turkish battleship.

"You're lucky I used my common sense and didn't buy it," I said. "By the way, my check for the piece hasn't arrived yet."

"We're not buying it."

"What's wrong?" I asked.

"Nothing happened," he said. "We told you to buy the battleship, but you didn't follow even that simple order."

Dazed, all I said was, "Yes."

"Yes, what?" asked the editor.

"Yes, sir."

Hoping all was not lost, I frantically called up Mr. Toker to tell him that I had been thinking it over and that I now agreed with him: the *Yavuz* was a wonderful ship. I wanted to buy it sight unseen.

"The ship is sold already," he said.

"To whom?" I asked suspiciously.

"The Italians. They bought the previous one also. They make razor blades out of the scrap."

Experiences like that have driven me to lecturing at colleges. My advice to anybody considering a career as a free-lance writer is: "Remember the *Yavuz*!"

# PART FIVE

# For $250,000 I Would Give All of This Up

In 1967, the editors of *Monocle* conducted a survey of members of the literary and other establishments on the question: Why did you (or did you not) sell out? I was invited to write a socio-political interpretation of the results of the survey. My own work in the field of selling out is perhaps too well known to go into. But I'm going to go into it anyway.

I have lived the life of a rather average mid-twentieth-century Northern New Jersey writer, i.e., one conspicuously free of rigidity to principle. As a result I can be accused of having sold out in almost every area possible. I want to limit my remarks to the one area in which I had never sold out, my craft as a freelance article writer.

In our business you have to publish or perish. Still I always wrote for myself. The one principle I had left to sell was that of writing only to amuse people, or to enlighten them, but never to mislead them.

I decided to sacrifice this remaining shred of integrity. Like Ayn Rand working in a steel mill as background for her novel, *Atlas Shrugged*, or George Plimpton playing for the Detroit Lions, I took a job at an advertising agency in order to become an authority on selling out.

Madison Avenue, the legendary place the poet Milne* sang of when he wrote:

> *He*
> *climbed*
> *and*
> *he*
> *climbed*
> *and*
> *he*
> *climbed,*
> *and*
> *as*
> *he*
> *climbed,*
> *he*
> *sang*
> *a*
> *little*
> *song*
> *to*
> *himself.*
> *It*
> *went*

* A. A. Milne, 1926.

*like*
*this:*

> *Isn't it funny*
> *How a bear likes honey?*
> *Buzz! Buzz! Buzz!*
> *I wonder why he does?*

Madison Avenue, the place which probably has the highest incidence of selling out per square foot in America!

Bruno Bettelheim wrote:

If one is to fully understand a psychological state one must be capable of considerable empathy tempered by critical judgment. Some people have deliberately subjected themselves to experiences that would enable them to gain empathy and introspect about the schizophrenic experience and permit others to study it objectively. Recent experiments with sensory deprivation belong in this class. Others have used drugs and induce psychotic-like states in themselves and possibly something of value may be learned from them, too, though I doubt it. But all studies of this kind exclude the one factor that I believe makes an experience extreme: its inescapability.

To know one can interrupt an experiment at will keeps the experience from being totally overwhelming. . . .

It worried me that my sacrifice might be taken as lightly as Bruno Bettelheim would take a social scientist who hoped to learn all about prostitution by playing a piano in a whorehouse. But the literary establishment, I'm happy to say, took me seriously. "Did you hear," somebody at a publisher's cocktail party told me a week after I had started working on Madison Avenue, "Kitman sold out to advertising."

"I'm Kitman," I explained to the embarrassed fellow.

Most of my favorite authors had sold out at some time in their careers. Nathaniel Hawthorne, for example, wrote a campaign biography of James L. Polk. I read extensively in Hobbes, the founding father of philosophical materialism, and found that he had very little to say about the economics of selling out in the modern world.

Hobbes said, "As in other things, so in men, not the seller, but the buyer determines the price; for let a man (as most men do) rate themselves at the highest value they can get, their true value is more than is esteemed by others." The first thing I learned is that Hobbes is irrelevant on Madison Avenue. You are roughly what you dream you are worth. Since the price a man sells out for is very important, I'd like to go into this in some detail.

In October 1967, when I began the research, I had been selling articles regularly to the highest-paying free-lance magazine writers' markets, i.e., *Playboy* and the *Saturday Evening Post*. I was earning roughly $1.25 an hour, or so it seemed to my wife. While my fee per article was very high, her time-and-motion studies showed that I was one of the slowest free-lance writers in America. Whatever the fee for an article, it always worked out to what your average free-lance migratory worker earned.

The first time an agency asked how much money I needed in the way of salary, I was too embarrassed to tell them the truth. Every man has his price, Sir Robert Walpole once said.

So I quoted my neighbor's: an outrageous sum of ten thousand dollars.

Later I learned that I was way out of line. Nobody hired a copywriter for as little as ten thousand dollars on Madison Avenue today. But Daniel Stern, the novelist who sells out as a vice president at McCann-Ericson, called back an hour later with the good news that he could hire me at that figure.

At lunch, Martin Solow, the president of Solow/Wexton, another Madison Avenue agency, asked the same question. I nervously tried to change the subject. "Are you happy?" I asked. "For $250,000 I would give all this up," he said. Wondering whether that was before or after taxes, I shut my eyes and added five thousand dollars to the early-morning quotation. He said that was fine.

At my third interview, after lunch, at Carl Ally, Inc., I swallowed hard and tacked on another five thousand. "That is a little high," the president and creative director observed drily, "since you've never written an ad in your life. How do you know you can do it?"

"Your money back," I said, "if not completely satisfied." In my nervousness, I threw around a lot of outlandish claims about the product I was selling, capping it off with a double-or-nothing offer. The executive, who took pride in his ability to judge talent, looked me straight in the eye and decided that I was only kidding.

Actually I didn't know if I could write an ad. Kitman's law on selling out is: never sell yourself short. As Mr. Justice Blackburn's decision, in *Smith* v. *Hughes* (1871), ran: "Whatever may be the case in the court of morals, there is no legal obligation on the vendor to inform the purchaser that he is under mistake, not induced by the act of the vendor." I was hired for the third time that day.

Within five or six hours, my price on the open market had doubled. If I had fully understood the mechanics of the marketplace, I would have gone on to a fourth agency and accepted a job at twenty-five thousand, a fifth agency at thirty thousand, and so on, until I had priced myself out of the senior-copywriter market, and been kicked upstairs into the board room of some agency where you don't have to know how to write an ad.

I weighed the three job offers in hand, taking the usual factors into consideration, such as which offered the greatest challenge, and picked the one that paid the most money. Naturally I wouldn't have been offered a dime at one of your average Madison Avenue agencies, like J. Walter Thompson. I had gone directly to the market for my offbeat talent. You can't sell out, no matter what your price, where there's no market for your commodity.

Carl Ally, Inc., took pride in its being a creative, as they say in the business, "shop," which did experimental things, like hiring inexperienced writers for their major accounts. The agency's major contribution to advertising history, before hiring me, was its famous war for Hertz against Avis.

Until Carl Ally got the account, Hertz turned the other cheek to Avis's claims that it tried harder because it was only No. 2 in the car-rental field. In the winter of 1966 and the spring of 1967, Ally stunned the ad world with a campaign which explained why Hertz was No. 1. In one of those little-known ironies which can only happen in wartime, I had been assigned by *Harper's* to be a kind of war correspondent in covering the Hertz-Avis fight. At my current rate of production, I would have gotten to the story in 1973 (Martin Mayer ground out the piece instead in the spring of 1968). Suddenly I found myself a combatant: the senior writer on the Hertz account.

At first I thought I had made a mistake, since nobody at the agency thought he was selling out. Apparently on Madison Avenue you don't sell out unless you leave a creative shop for a higher salary at an uncreative shop.

Carl Ally himself is a forty-three-year-old former World War II bomber pilot who spent most of his time flying around the country looking for new business. One of the first inter-office memos I got paid for reading urged other people to fly the company plane; otherwise the agency would be forced to sell it. He often invited his associates to fly with him, but there seemed to be a reluctance to go along. I later learned that he caught up on his reading while at the controls.

I thought he was an advertising genius. He told me this himself several times before I went to work on the Hertz account.

One of his theories about great advertising is that it should never lie to people. By telling the truth, ads hit people hard. We had to go out there and slug Avis in the marketplace. We had to kick Avis all over Madison Avenue, leave them bleeding at the counters in the airports, crush the sonsofbitches, let them know they had been in a mean fight. That's the way my new boss talked.

When it came time to present my thoughts

**265**

on advertising in the first few conferences with the Hertz creative team, I told my new colleagues: "We have to go out there and slug Avis in the marketplace, kick them all over Madison Avenue, leave them bleeding at the counters in the airports, crush the Avis sonsofbitches." Basically, I told them everything Carl had told me, adding a few grisly embellishments of my own, such as using nuclear weapons where it hurts. I was ready to go to war with the enemy, Avis, again.

At first my colleagues eyed me suspiciously. They thought I was tough competition. But eventually I found the other creative people on the account were pacifists. They didn't want another war. They wanted to do different advertising, great advertising. Otherwise they couldn't live with themselves: they would be selling out. Obviously we were in advertising for different reasons.

The strategy the doves planned to follow was finding the good points about Hertz's position, *vis-à-vis* Avis, and writing to these advantages, and by implication saying that Avis was inferior. I spent the first few days reading all the relevant market research and the ads from the war years, looking for some of these points of superiority.

It seemed to me that Avis really tried harder. The more I studied the car-rental business the more my pro-Avis sympathies rose. Essentially there appeared to be no major difference between the No. 1 and No. 2 car-rental companies, except that Hertz was owned by RCA and Avis by IT&T. Why not give the little fellow a break?

As part of my research I rented a Hertz car for the first time. The ashtray filled with cigars fell on the floor of the car. The girl at the counter said that if I didn't want the car a lot of other people did; she was a very busy woman. This sort of thing happens periodically in the car-rental business. Sometimes you have a good experience; sometimes you don't.

I came back to the office with a great new idea about how the agency could get more people to rent Hertz cars, which Carl said was our goal. Take the eight million dollars in the ad budget and pump it back into the business. Pay the counter girls more, so the company will be able to attract a politer class of workers to deal with the public; spend more on servicing the cars so there'll be fewer breakdowns, and so forth. My colleagues listened to all of this in stony silence; then they laughed. There didn't seem to be anything in it for the agency.

I went back to my office, closed the door, and started writing my first letter of resignation:

DEAR CARL:

By the time you read this, I will be at Doyle, Dane Bernbach [the Avis agency at the time].

I have decided to defect to Avis as a matter of principle. I will ask Bill Bernbach for asylum and should he refuse to grant it I will chain myself to Bernbach's secretary.

Please don't try to call me to talk me out of what I have to do if I am to live with myself. I will be accepting only calls from Phil Dougherty [the advertising columnist of *The New York Times*] to explain my position. I will call you sometime.

Your agency's secret strategy for the new campaign is safe with me.

It was nice knowing you, even so briefly.

Sincerely,
Marvin Kitman

Hopefully Bernbach would hire me because all my experience—two days—was in the car-rental field. I already had worked out a great new campaign for Avis, which consisted of a few bars of familiar music and the slogan: "Let *Avis* put you in the driver's seat."

But I couldn't go through with it. I had come to Madison Avenue to sell out, not to save my integrity. In the next seven months I wrote about a dozen advertisements and radio commercials and one thirty-second television commercial which never went on the air (it had first-act problems). The major theme of this work was that Crap is Good.

It was the most satisfying corruption I had ever experienced. I finally made *The New Yorker* with something I had written, even if it was only a 150-word "article," as I called the ads to the end.

This is not to say that there wasn't friction between myself as a sellout and those who felt they weren't selling out. I still remember looking at the first thing I had ever written under the influence of money. That's an example of really commercial writing, I thought proudly. The creative director said it was pretty good, too. He tinkered with it—"cleaning up the copy a little," he explained—and eventually six of the four hundred words found their way into print, five of which were: "Hertz. *We can help a little.*" That was the campaign's slogan.

I didn't complain. Sellouts have their principles too, and an important one is profit without honor.

Later it was explained to me that what I actually was doing in this case was copping out. The true sellout would have cried: "That's reprehensible! You've emasculated what I wanted to say by cutting out those 394 words. You've taken the heart out of my message to the consumers. I've had it at this shop. I quit."

Then, instead of walking out, you stay at your post.

I had been hired to bring a fresh point of view into advertising, and not surprisingly I did come up with a number of good ideas, most of which dealt with increasing the dignity of the profession. I suggested, for example, that ads be signed by writers. Since it was such a controversial step, and the agency might not want to become totally committed to it, I offered to let them use only my name as a test, provided they would include the agate line, "The views of the agency are not necessarily those of the writer."

Most of the other ideas are too technical to go into here. I will mention one, however, in some detail because it illustrates a classic case of selling out.

My major contribution to the art of advertising writing was the idea of treating commercials as a serious art form. For some time, the television critics had been saying that the commercials were the only things worth watching on the networks. When Carl Ally told me that a new Hertz spot (which I had not yet seen) featuring an efficiency expert was "the greatest commercial of all time," I suggested that we give it the full treatment.

"THE EFFICIENCY EXPERT"
SOON TO BE RELEASED AS A MAJOR
TELEVISION COMMERCIAL

was the headline in the full page I prepared for *The New York Times* television section. "Gala Premiere Tonight (December 21, 1967). See the sixty-second commercial in its entirety beginning at 10:29 on NBC-TV. Also playing *The Dean Martin Show*."

The ad showed coming attractions from the commercial. It also included out-of-context quotes from the critics who attended a screening I had used my influence with the literary establishment to arrange the week before (Sam Blum of *Redbook* called it ". . . Promising . . ."; Wilfrid Sheed, the *Esquire* film critic, said ". . . Four umlauts . . .").

"If you can spare a minute," the advertisement ended, "see this important documentary commercial tonight. Should you be unable to attend the premiere of *The Efficiency Expert*, don't worry. Like most great works of commercial art, it will be shown again, again and again."

It was my misfortune to have had this idea used for calling attention to a commercial which should have been hidden.

For those who missed it, *The Efficiency Expert* was a mildly satirical story about how Hertz hired a man who had dedicated his life to efficiency to eliminate all the bugs in the car-rental business. "Businessman," the narrator began this epic, which second for second cost more to produce than *Cleopatra* (sixty

270

thousand dollars), "perhaps you have been noticing that Hertz is ticking away like a fine watch lately. This is no accident. . . ."

It went on to explain the new speedy writing range where the counter girls were trained to fill out rental forms faster and various other innovations this machine-like man had introduced to get the cars into the hands of renters faster, faster. It ended on the hilarious note: "And why? Why are we doing all of this? . . . I don't know why. I'm only following orders."

The narrator was an actor named Sorrel Brooke who carried a riding crop, wore a full-length leather coat, rimless glasses, and shiny black boots which he clicked in a Germanic manner from time to time. I sensed immediately that he was going to be a controversial figure in noncontroversial commercial television.

True men of integrity would have quit on the spot. It was the most anti-German commercial ever made, and the West German cultural affairs attaché could be expected to lodge a stern protest against the blatant use of German stereotypes. In jest, I told the creative director of the Hertz account, who had dreamed up the commercial, "If anybody complains, say he's a typical Swiss."

When the rough cut came into the shop, we were all summoned to the screening room to view it with Carl Ally. He pounded the table happily as he watched it the first time. "It has thrust," he said. "Play it again." We were forced to sit through *The Efficiency Expert* six times. That's only six minutes, but it seemed like an hour. As I heard Ally explaining this was the greatest commercial of all time for the sixth time, I tried to think of some sneaky way to work an attack on Hertz's Japanese customers, who rented a lot of cars on the West Coast, into my commercial about returning car keys.

*The Efficiency Expert was* a great commercial, in the sense that a new miracle drug for curing a cold would be great, if it didn't have the side effect of causing a few cases of blindness. It seemed so obvious that there would be the side effect of reminding some viewers of concentration camps, that I didn't even mention it. I was on Madison Avenue to sell out, not to carry on my old ways as a bleeding heart, kneejerk-liberal writer. By writing this ad in *The New York Times*—my only connection with this whole project, I want to emphasize again—I was being true to myself as a sellout, that is, only following orders.

The commercial had one of the highest viewer ratings in television history (helped along not only by my ad but by the appearance of Frank Sinatra on Dino's Christmas show).

A few listeners, as I predicted, complained about the commercial. Maybe a thousand called in to the network within two minutes after the curtain went down on *The Efficiency Expert.* By 9:05 A.M. the next morning, perhaps another two thousand people called into Hertz corporate headquarters. All happened to be Jewish.

"Just a drop in the bucket," I said happily. "Wait till the Germans realize in a month or so we were poking fun at them. This one has thrust in two directions."

Hertz was very disturbed by the trickle of credit cards which flowed into its executive

272

offices from enraged Jewish internationalist bankers that second morning. But Ally favored running the commercial again, again and again. As I explained to the nervous people on the account who once loved the commercial, "The secret of success in advertising is repetition."

The third day the reviews really poured in. It was a critical success, everybody seemed to agree, but a commercial failure. The agency spent the full day in conference, about what to say to the client. "Our laughing stock is up," I summarized the situation as I saw it, "but our corporate stock is down. What's more important?"

Approximately six million people saw the commercial. When the number of complaints reached a mere ten thousand, Ally began losing faith in the greatest commercial in the world. "All you have to do is change the ending a little," I said in a last-ditch fight to save it, "Have one of the Hertz Fords hit that sonofabitch Nazi." Ally said, in effect, it was a free country. Everybody, including the .7 percent of the television audience who didn't like the commercial, had the right to his opinion, and he was taking it off the air.

Heretofore I had admired Carl Ally as a real person. He wasn't like those fancy Madison Avenue phonies who thought that what a man wore was important. But now I admired him for the humility with which he was able to throw out his idea of what was great. The average Madison Avenue chief executive would have protected his integrity, i.e., always thinking of the client first, by killing the commercial the first day. But Ally agonized over it for three days. He was a Christ-like figure until he finally decided to save the account and the agency.

As great as Ally was at that beautiful moment in his career, he was nothing compared to the Hertz and RCA executives who had put awesome pressure on my hero to get that offensive piece of racist junk off the air. In the highest level of management, both Hertz and RCA have an unusually high percentage of Jews and former Jews (Unitarians). At every stage of production, they saw that the commercial was making fun of an Eichmann-like figure who quoted directly from the Jerusalem trials to make its comic point. Why in the name of God didn't they intercede? I explained to my colleagues later this was an example of Jewish self-hatred.

From time to time, one of the soap companies gets the bright idea to put out a new detergent called *Drek*. The Jewish executives are so busy denying their past in these pseudo-Christian companies that they completely forget what the word means. The product is just about ready to go on the market when in the spirit of brotherhood some Quaker tells the Jewish advertising manager that the product's name may offend some consumers.

By not recognizing the obnoxious qualities of *The Efficiency Expert*, the Hertz-RCA management was denying its Jewish consciousness and in effect they were subliminally inviting self-punishment.

That's how Norman Podhoretz might have interpreted the episode. As far as I was concerned, the Hertz and RCA managements were selling out as businessmen. It seemed to me they were ignoring the unique selling proposition in the commercial: if it enraged a small number of Jewish customers, it also appealed to the latent anti-Semitism widespread in the halls of top management, where most of the car-rental business is.

All of this latent anti-Semitism which Hertz unleashed in the country, I might add in passing, eventually came home to roost in the filibuster in the U.S. Senate which kept Justice Abe Fortas from fulfilling his destiny as the first Jewish Chief Justice of the Supreme Court.

*The Efficiency Expert* also affected my career. As the months passed I gradually was given all the credit for it. In some way the feeling grew that I had conceived, written, art-directed and even scored (incidental music from Wagner's *Götterdämmerung*) this sixty-second powerful social documentary. It was on my reel, as they say. The way my old comrades in arms began avoiding me, I assumed my days in advertising were numbered, as indeed they were.

My mother thought that I had gone to Madison Avenue to learn a trade: deep down, everybody at the agency assumed that I had come to write a book about them. I denied it, of course: I only planned to write an introduction to a book about them. If they had asked if I was planning to write an introduction, I wouldn't have denied it.

Every two weeks or so Carl Ally would stop by my office and ask how the book was going. He even referred to it in conferences. I remember the day he attacked everybody in the Hertz creative group for trying to destroy him by doing such soft-sell ads. He pounded Amil Gargano's beautiful new conference table at us sonsofbitches and shouted other obscenities. Then he glared at me: "And you can put that in your book!" Which I interpreted loosely as permission for using all these anecdotes.

By June, he began to suspect that I really wasn't doing a book about him. Not even an article for *The New York Times Magazine*.

If Ally had been familiar with Bruno Bettelheim, he would have understood why I wasn't a great advertising man. The experience wasn't totally overwhelming, as Bettelheim predicted, because I knew I could escape.

I wasn't making the quick changes of thought necessary to get ahead in the advertising business. I hadn't developed an ulcer. Obviously I wasn't giving it my all, which I imagine Ally expected. But he probably also expected that in my time away from the office I would be churning out lengthy learned articles about him for *Atlantic, Harper's* and *Partisan Review*. Everybody could tell by my fatigue that I was writing at night. Even then it wouldn't have mattered if I had been writing about Carl Ally.

In the seven months on Madison Avenue, not a word of mine appeared in print about Carl Ally. Life was grim enough at the office without my earning $1.25 an hour writing about it at home.

In July 1968, Carl finally decided I was a luxury as just an adman; he wasn't getting his money's worth. After a lengthy, agonizing apology about how a medium-sized agency couldn't afford a resident guru, he terminated my job.

For $250,000 I would work on Madison Avenue again.

# INDEX

AN INDEX is a vestigial organ like an appendix. Anything that encourages the reading of select passages of a book, when the author meant for it to be read in its entirety, should come out. As an experiment in publishing science, I am using the space reserved for the index as a guide to source materials.

Marie Torre of the *New York Herald Tribune* went to jail rather than reveal her sources. But I am proud of the people who helped shape my writings. If it was a crime to have stolen their ideas, some may have concluded by reading this far into the book, it was only petty larceny. However, the ideas were the best my sources were capable of.

The index to the great thoughts others have had during the three-year period (1966-1969) I wrote this book is not always reliable. In some cases I have forgotten who told me what and given duplicate credit. Sometimes more than one person had the same idea. Space limitations prevent mentioning all the contributors of some of the most familiar jokes. By inference, every idea not credited to some other individual is original thinking by the author.

Still it is the most successful analysis of sources used by the author ever undertaken. Hopefully, it will inspire other more important authors to tell the truth about where they got their material.